Awakening to Love

A Channeled Book about our Spiritual Relationship to
Consciousness, Universal Love and Awareness.

SIMON HERFET

Interior Illustration by Isabella Herfet.

Contents

Interior Illustration by Isabella Herfet (aged 9).

Preface

'Let me use a very simple analogy just for a moment, before we start this book. Think of a light bulb, it shines brightly for a period of time and then it goes 'ping'. It shines no more. It dies. Many people, I think, see their life or their body in a similar way. That we are here just for a short period of time and then we are gone. When the truth of the matter, I believe, is that we are in fact the electricity, which passes through and radiates us all. Which animates and links us all together, with a conscious 'loving' awareness shared by us all. Rather than just the light bulb itself. This is what in brief, the following questions and answers are about, a 'chat' if you like, between me and the 'electricity' that I do believe we all share. So please do read on and I hope you too, may have a 'light-bulb' moment about your own true self.'

This book had been 'gestating' in my mind for many years and I always knew what the essence of the message would be about. However, I did not know the format, which it might take. Indeed - for many years in fact, I thought that it might take the form of a novel but a suitable story never came into my mind. A format of questions and answers turned out to be the result.

Initially, I had some misgivings about this method of relaying the type of information that I wished to share for various reasons but in the end, this type of format felt like a natural choice for me too. The reasons for which, will be explained more fully later in the text.

Anyone briefly surveying the method through which this

information is relayed, to a part of my consciousness, by some greater aspect of 'self', which is, I believe shared by all beings, could perhaps still be excused for thinking that the method of access to the information is somewhat questionable. However, as the writer, all I can say in my own defence, not surprisingly, is that I trust wholly in the process; and the essential truth of the nature and content of the information, brought forth in this way.

At the end of the day, much of our great art, literature and music, is, I believe, 'channeled' by the individuals concerned from somewhere; sometimes from seemingly outside of their own self.

During my life, one of the most useful skills, which I have learnt, is meditation, this practice has helped me in so many ways. It is primarily, I believe, the method which has helped me the most to develop the ability to bring through this information. Maybe though, it is also a gift, with which I was born. Irrespectively, my main wish is to use it to help others and so in relaying this information to a world in which a multitude of people are suffering from a 'spiritual famine', I do hope at least, some of the information contained in this book will help to either dispel or diminish such hunger.

Regarding the content of this message, I ask the reader to listen to their own intuition as much as possible - as they read the information delivered here - to whether the information is acceptable to themselves and if not of course, to simply move on to whatever resonates more with their own truth.

Finally, I should clarify the meaning of the initials 'S.H.', for they represent the initials of the author (these denoting my questions) and those of 'H.S.', represent the term 'Higher-Self' (denoting the answers given to me) which I whole heartedly believe to be the source of the replies to my questions. The essence and a description of the meaning of the term 'Higher-Self' is contained later in the dialogue. All that I will add at this juncture, is to say that, the awareness that is yours reading these words, is in fact the same shared awareness I believe, which at the deepest level, channeled the replies to the questions revealed in this book. In fact, for that matter every other book ever written. This is because, we all share the same ocean of consciousness which not only created us all, but also sustains 'ALL THAT IS'.

Dedication

This book is dedicated to my wife Sarah and to my children Daniel, Rebekah, Tommy and Isabella.

November 2017.

Introduction

H.S. "You have been drawn to this book for a reason. The reason is because you wish to seek something within yourself to explain many of your unanswered questions about the true nature of your being. You are on a tide of change and that tide is carrying many others along with yourself on a similar journey.

This is a time of great awakening to those aspects of your being, which have been hidden from you, for so long. Your soul's call, is your own wishful thinking for something better in life, to that which you already think you know to be real. This book has been written for you, by an awareness shared with you at the deepest level of your being. This is quite simply because all of humanity; all of creation in your universe shares the same consciousness. This of course does not mean, you are all equally aware, as you know this is not the case. Let us suppose for a moment that you have lived at least one life on Earth before. Somewhere deep inside of your memory bank there is a flicker of remembrance of some of that life which you lived. You probably would not associate it as being a past life recall, but more likely a memory of something you read once somewhere, or a memory from a movie, or a television programme you had perhaps once viewed. This is because your logical mind tries its best to place your thoughts in alignment with the beliefs you hold about the purpose of life- as you see it to be.

Yet the purpose of life is for it to be a journey to a deeper understanding of your place here.

Why were you born into a human body?

What are you at the deepest level and how might you be connected to others in some sort of spiritual way?

Until you begin to expand, into the consciousness which you share with all creation, you cannot know your true self or your place in creation. The emptiness you may feel inside of yourself, is we would suggest symptomatic of the denial of the truth of who you really are.

If you look in to the mirror my friends and see for once with an open heart who you really are. Are you not the consciousness staring back at yourself? This is the wisdom inherent within every cell of your being and far, far beyond. For it is the same wisdom which created your sun, your moon, your planet and every other galaxy, including your own. The one in which you now dwell.

It is time to continue your awakening to the ocean of your true being. You are the wave and the ocean, staring into the mirror back at yourself and into the abyss of that part of your being which has denied this truth for too long. Awaken now, like a child from your slumber into the sunlight and the radiance and the love which is your birth right and the power behind your every thought and action. Now, in your awakening but one being can emerge, for it was only ever one consciousness which lightly slept in your human slumber."

one

A Starting Point

H.S. "Whichever way you look. In fact, whatever the profession you choose in life, you must ask yourself this question, "Why do I choose that?"

"Why do I choose to do this job?"

"What are my inclinations about it. What will it bring me? What will it give to the world? Why should I do it?"

This is not a selfish synopsis. This is not a reason to delay. But, when you ask these sorts of questions it frees the mind from doubt about one's own motivation to motivate others. For to motivate others, we ourselves need to be motivated, you see. Unless we ourselves are motivated by the project at hand it simply will not reach fruition.

So, Firstly, let us look at your motivation my son.

What is the true reason you want to write this book?"

S.H. "I want to feel truly successful at something and I want to help the world be a better place."

H.S. "Okay that is fine and honourable.

Why don't you feel successful already, as there is much you have already achieved in your life?"

S.H. "Yes, but I am not sure I have done yet, that which will be my greatest success."

H.S. "Which is what?"

S.H. "To complete this book and bring it into realisation and help the world."

H.S. "Okay, how will it help the world?"

S.H. "By making some people see and believe that they are all part of the creator of all that is and therefore be kinder and more loving to others".

H.S. "Yes, okay very honourable. Do you really believe that?"

S.H. "Yes."

H.S. "Do you think it could change the world or just the lives of a few?"

S.H. "A few yes, but even a tiny change is a change. To change one person's viewpoint and life is a change. Be it a small one."

H.S. "Indeed it is."

S.H. "What is the point of this question?"

H.S. "The point is for you my son to realise that who you are, is who you are. You cannot change who you are. What you can do is awaken to who you are. There is no change involved in the 'true' person you see. The idea or belief that you can change someone is an error. That is a simple but very fundamental point. Keep the energy of that thought or idea close and always remember the point is to 'awaken' and not to 'change' the individual whoever they are. Do you see?"

S.H. "Yes, I think so."

H.S. "To put it another way. If you seek always to change people you will always fail. But if you seek always to awaken, then you will succeed more often. What the world needs now is to 'awaken', not change first. Awakening happens, followed by change. Do you see? This is a very simple but very important premise. It is a fundamental truth."

S.H. "Thank you."

H.S. "Okay, so having shown you that it is about 'awakening', not changing first. Then the focus, the energy, the intent of the message is on the 'awakening' process.
How do we do that?
I ask your question for you."

S.H. "What must be done is to write something that has the ring of truth and love about it. When joy is created, it is most often because truth has been shared in those words and an opening of the heart has happened in the individual. The words are 'heart-felt' to use an often-used phrase. Words from the heart so to speak. A distant memory has been released from its slumber. A dark recess of the brain has been opened and something has been set free. When in fact we have freed own 'true' self.
For in truth we are consciousness confined by a body until we set it free through the knowledge of who we truly are.
So, I have been trying to think of a title for this book for ages. I was going to call it 'Love is the key'. Now I am thinking of calling it 'Awakening to change'. What do you think?"

H.S. "Is the purpose of awakening, to change?
Or is it an 'awakening', just that?
Does an awakening need to have a purpose?"

S.H. "I suppose not. An awakening is just that. An awakening".

H.S. "Yes, indeed. Change obviously is going to come in various ways for different people. 'Love is the Key', is a different proposition again. There are many human connotations around the word 'Love'. Such as love is the key to what? I know you mean spiritual truth and peace. That is true. Different titles have a different effect on different people. How about 'Awakening to Love'?"

S.H. "Yes, I like that. The emphasis is on the 'awakening', rather than the slightly bland multi-dimensional term 'love'. Another way of saying 'Awakening is the Key', though it doesn't have the same ring to it. Maybe, 'Awakening to all that is'. Though I feel a bit like a plagiarist with that title."

H.S. "Truth is truth. There is no copyright on it!"

S.H. "Yes indeed. I like 'Awakening to Love' it has the joint energy of two very powerful words in my opinion.
By the way I am enjoying this dialogue. Who is it with by the way. Is it God?
Is it my higher self?
Or is it just my imagination?"

H.S. "My son, there is no division. To use your often-used analogy of the ocean of being. If a drop of water in the ocean could speak to another droplet, who would be speaking to who? It would in fact be the ocean sharing information with itself. Likewise, that is what is occurring here! It keeps the point very clear that there is no division between us whatsoever. There is no you and me, or me and it. There is just one. I only. As is the ocean, only one."

S.H. "Is it unusual or rare to have the ability to have this sort of mental dialogue?"

H.S. "Yes and no. Many have and can do this. A greater many cannot. Their main fear, is that to do so would indicate that maybe they are crazy. You are not crazy. You do not fear the process and you know it is possible and you have awakened to who you truly are, several years ago my son. This does not make you special however, so always remember that. It is a gift if you like. But one that you are still learning to perfect."

S.H. "I am still not sure about this book, i.e. is it going to be a novel or a series of dialogues with the rest of the ocean. Ha, ha!"

H.S. "It can be whatever you want it to be. Whatever you feel most comfortable with really. It is your own choice. You must decide on that."

S.H. "Which is most likely to be successful in awakening the most people?"

H.S. "That depends on the content on either or, i.e. which one you choose to write about".

S.H. "Can't I have the heads up?"

H.S. "Choose the one which gives the most satisfaction. Which you enjoy most. Where most energy flows to sustain the story and yourself through the process".

S.H. "This seems easier to me than story writing. But, I do feel it's been done already in the 'Conversations with God' books!"

H.S. "Sure, I understand that. This is however a way for you to check in and ask for advice and question yourself and your motives about this process though, don't you think?"

S.H. "Yes I do. I find it hard to totally surrender to write a novel which is channeled. When I have no idea about the narrative, in case it is rubbish and I lose the thread of it while writing it."

H.S. "Trust in the process!"

two

Love, What is it All About?

S.H. "What is this awakening to love business?"

H.S. "Well it is not a business that is for sure!"

S.H. "Is it a process or is it a natural event?"

H.S. "Like a flower opening to the sunshine when its time is due, the knowingness within the flower 'knows' when it is time to open its petals. It does not need 'telling,' it is a natural process. So, 'yes,' then it is also a process.

"How does it come about though, with and for human beings, this awakening? This deep spiritual flower latent within all humans. And when the flower does open what beauty does it radiate to the beholder?

What does a flower do other than radiate beauty to humans?

It attracts bees to help pollinate and it can in some species release seeds which lead to new growth of another similar flower.

So, when our consciousness opens eventually, then we feel more of our own inner beauty and wisdom and we radiate it out to the world and those others around us, so that perhaps like the self-seeding process, we also help the flower of consciousness spread. As

7

it spreads to others, beauty and peace and so comfort is spread far and wide."

S.H. "Can another be awakened at any time or only when they are ready to awaken?"

H.S. "My son, the answer is this; as a flower opens when the conditions are right, so with the individual. A flower in most cases knows not to open in times inclement. So, it is with the individual. The time of awakening is different for all. The process and cause is different for many, though not all. It is as beautiful to behold for the almighty and the individual as it is for the flower. The time of awakening affects many aspects of the individual, which of course lead eventually to many changes within them. These are changes physical, spiritual, emotional and mental, all for the good of the health of the individual. The awakening of another therefore cannot be forced it will happen always at the right time for them!"

S.H. "What is the purpose of life?"

H.S. "You explained it beautifully only yesterday when you yourself explained it to the man you spoke to at the harbour. It is to awaken to who you truly are. Which is God."

S.H. "So, I am God".

H.S. "Yes my son. You are God. You all are God. You may doubt it. You may change your mind often. But this does not alter the truth of who you are, or who you ever were, at the essence of your being. Your beauty radiates from within you like a bright star visible to all. Not just in this world but the one beyond. Trust in your beauty. Trust in your own goodness. As well as that of all others you meet. For even the most evil and wicked, as they might be perceived, are 'God' also. Yet asleep to the fact, of who they truly are!"

S.H. "Why is there so much trouble and strife still in this world?"

H.S. "My son when has there not been. In your brief life, yes, brief to date. Has this not always appeared to be the case?"

S.H. "Yes."

H.S. "It is the nature of the game for those who live asleep to the truth of who they truly are. They are like children with eyes to see but refusing to use them. People thinking, they are blind when they are not. Groping in the dark for their way forwards. People only see what they want to see. They only believe what they want to believe. They are afraid to open their minds to a greater reality. To a reality which does not fit in with the belief system of others and the public at large. You my son, have found the courage to believe in a reality other than the one you have been trained to see as the truth. It can feel scary and even irresponsible to begin with. Perhaps, 'I am crazy', you think sometimes to yourself, to have such way-out ideas, of who you truly are or might be. To say you are 'God'. Most people will think you are, at least a little crazy. Will they not?

Keep having the courage and faith to believe it and you will have power to change the world through your own small actions and writing. More people than you currently think or believe will one day read these simple words. And many will have an 'awakening' to who they truly are, themselves. You then, will have fulfilled the true service and purpose of why you chose to incarnate at this time my son."

three

The Courage to Love

H.S. "It takes courage my son to love - to truly love- my son.

Not just others but your own self, too.

You see, to love another is a risk of sorts. For to do so, you are opening yourself up to the possibility of hurt and rejection. Are you not?"

S.H. "Yes, I guess so. That has been my experience, on occasion."

H.S. "Indeed my son, but through the experience of loving another, did it not also bring many riches for your soul?

Did it not also help you yourself open up to theirs in a way you previously had not found possible within yourself?"

S.H. "Yes."

H.S. "So the gain was worth the pain?"

S.H. "Yes."

H.S. "You cannot move forward in any way without love. Love is the energy of all creation. Every action, every thought indeed."

S.H. "So, if every deed, as you say requires love as its source. That must include evil deeds too?"

H.S. "Only in as much as love provides free choice. Free choice to commit either good or bad. The choice is yours or the individuals, whoever that may be. God's gift is free choice. If you did not have free choice, then where would that leave you?

It would be like locking a person as they grow up into an adult in a house. How would they learn?

No learning from experience equals no growth.

Free choice = Growth=Awakening. Ultimately.

This point is one that so many people struggle with and why so many refuse to believe in God when they see so much cruelty in the world. It occurs because humanity have the choice to do as they choose to do. Do you see?"

S.H. "Yes, free choice is necessary, otherwise we as individuals and humanity as a whole would not grow in consciousness, ultimately."

H.S. "Yes, my son. As has already been pointed out to you, the purpose of life is to awaken to who you truly are. Which is God. God is all there is. That is consciousness. You are consciousness experiencing life in a human body. But you are not the body. You are not the mind. You are consciousness personified. Yet, you are not the person. You and all others are much more than that. Without limitation. You are the ocean. Not the 'droplet in the ocean', as you yourself often say.

From the day you were born, you identify with your own body. It begins even as a new born, for your body feels pain etc. and so the body identification begins. It is difficult not to identify with the body when you are indeed encased within one for so long as a lifetime. Is that not so my son?"

S.H. "Yes, that is so."

H.S. "And yet the body is a very remarkable creation, is it not? It is still barely understood. It's true function still not discovered by your science."

S.H. "What is its true function then. Is it not to discover why we are here and that we are God as you already explained?"

H.S. "No, my son. It is to love! To express love entirely, for God to inhabit a physical universe with humanity fully awake, rather than asleep. That is the reason I created the physical universe so that I could experience it in an awakened state. But for me to experience that fully I must wait for humanity to completely wake up. I have infinite time. So, there is no hurry you see."

S.H. "What is it that stops most people from raising their consciousness to the point that they wake up to all of this then?"

H.S. "My son there are many."

S.H. "I think I should ask at this point and probably I should have done so earlier- Why do you call me 'my son'?"

H.S. "It is because you are of course, as indeed you are all my creation. Simple.

To get back to the question- 'what is it that stops most people from raising their own consciousness'? The answer is, apathy. Because, they do not want too. They are hypnotised by the material world. By their own minds. That they are of it and limited to it! Yet they are not, of course not. By changing their mind. Their belief systems, they will see they are not. They are not who they have been trained to believe who they are. To do so, would mean that those in positions of perceived power, would have to believe, that ultimately, they in turn would be letting go of that power and they do not want to do that. This even includes established religions. Though not all.

Buddhism is the closest to the truth as it does not preach a doctrine as such, it points towards a path. But not a set one. It points a finger in a direction to follow without a road or path to follow and no other religion does that my son.

In most cases religion limits the individual to just another belief system based on limiting your awareness of who you truly are, which is, consciousness. All that is. Most religions will not tell you that. If they did there would be no reason for them i.e. religions to exist."

S.H. "What else keeps us in the dark from discovering who we truly are?"

H.S. "Fear, my son, fear of the truth. Fear is the flip side of love. Fear and love are like light and dark. Without darkness, how would you know what light is. You need the contrast to know it. So, it is with fear and consciousness. Fear keeps you in unconsciousness and love takes you to consciousness. That is open. Fear closes you down. Fear shuts off your awareness and love opens it up. It is that simple, believe it or not my son.

Fear is very powerful, but love is even more powerful. When you are feeling love, there is no room for fear. Love is creation and fear is death, so to speak. One emotion starts things. The other ends them. I am trying to keep this all as simple as possible for others to understand my son.

But fear is like a veil with many faces, fear comes in all shapes and sizes for different people. Yet as the veil is just a shadow hiding what is beyond, fear is the same, the truth is still the truth. It is like something hiding the truth beyond. But as a veil can fall away, so can fear and what is hidden can be revealed. The task is to see beyond the faces of fear, whatever they be for the individual. To have the courage to push through the veil or the shadows of fear. They are in truth only shadows."

S.H. "Today I noticed again my pattern that when things seem to be going my way the old fears surface, like self-sabotage."

H.S. "This is just a pattern. As it began so it can end. It is about where your mental focus is at any one time. Keep it positive my son."

S.H. "How can I best help others to awaken and therefore change things for the better?"

H.S. "My son, you are talking here reference the content of this dialogue that is taking place. First you need to capture our conversations, if you like. Then eventually you <u>will</u> find a publisher. You have a lot of help do not <u>forget</u>. Next others must be led to the book. Then they must read and assimilate the information within it. Next, they must mentally digest it to understand it at the deepest level. Some will do this, some will not be able to accept the content within it. However, those that do accept it, will awaken and change according to their own level of understanding and desire to change. This part is not really your concern. It is commendable that you care so much about it. It is best recommended that once the book is out there, so to speak, you just release and let go of any expectation of success in this field and leave that to divine providence.

Everyone is at a different stage on their journey through life. Just as you are. Some desire change. Some do not. Some desire a small change in themselves, some a smaller one. Very few desire a big change and most people fear change for it implies sacrifice i.e. self-sacrifice which more often than not, implies letting go of different things. Whether this be people, jobs or material things.

However, one small change can lead to many much bigger things. What is it, you most want to see change?"

S.H. "The world. I want to see more peace. Less suffering. More equality and humanity itself, to be raised to a higher level of consciousness. I know that my book can only have a small effect regards this."

H.S. "To repeat from tiny acorns, mighty oaks will grow. Remember, a book is like a seed which can grow in the minds of all those who read it. The energy they take forward can move mountains. The potential for change from one positive book my son, is far more powerful than you might imagine. So, set no limitations on the potential of this exercise, my son."

S.H. "These are very encouraging words. Thank you.
Why is the awakening process more important, than a positive change within people?"

H.S. "Because the true change in the individual follows the awakening process. To put it another way, everybody is already awake, but they do not realise it. Like a person sleep walking is unaware they are sleep walking. So, a person who is not awake, is not aware that they are not awake. They think they are already awake. They do not know that they are not yet awake until they truly are. To use your own, experience my son, about a different matter. You have said to people previously, that you do not know you have become a man, until you truly become one. Is that not correct my son?"

S.H. "Yes, I have said that several times. I know what you mean."

H.S. "So it is with the process of awakening. The awakening that we speak of here, is the awakening to the essence of our soul or spirit, the 'God' within all if you like. This is a fundamental shift in consciousness when it occurs. It is a slightly different process for all. It is a letting go of all your pre-conditioning about who you have been led to believe that you are. You have been taught by others and self-taught that you are your mind and body. That the extent of yourself is limited to just that and that is false. It is a severe limitation of who you truly are.

In truth, you are the opposite. You are not the body. You are not the mind. YOU ARE CONSCIOUSNESS."

S.H. "It is very hard not to identify with the body and the mind. I try my best each day to remember that I am much more than the body."

H.S. "Remember my son, you are not the body. It is the point your consciousness is currently being projected from.

In the cinema, you look at the screen to watch the film. Yet the movie is projected from behind you, wherever the projector is located, is the source of the movie not the screen. So, it is with your mind. You believe reality is outside of yourself, yet in truth it comes from your mind. This is the seat of your consciousness while in the body. Yet your consciousness does not need the body to live or survive, for it is eternal."

S.H. "Can you define courage for me please?"

H.S. "Courage is your own answer to your own problems whatever they may be. When we face a problem, courage is normally what is called for to address it, be it at the deepest level. It is the source of our being, often untapped, though most required. You see my son, when there are difficulties to be faced, the easiest option is just to ignore the problem and hope it will go away. However, most of the time a change in our reaction is called for. We must address the issue in a different way. You are endeavouring not to drink alcohol for at least a year. On some level that involves making a change. Part of you is concerned whether or not, you can face that change. It feels to you like a certain pleasure is being removed from your life. This maybe so. But is it not the case that other more valuable pleasures will replace those you are concerned about missing out on."

S.H. "Yes, that is true. But I am not sure I am having to draw on courage for that."

H.S. "Does it not take courage to resist something you like when faced with others drinking alcohol and possibly ridiculing you for not doing so. You care about what others think of you, is that not correct?"

S.H. "Yes, I suppose so."

H.S. "Well in being prepared to face that, is just one example of your courage and I could give you many more. Even if it seems to be a small challenge to you, my son. To many who regularly drink alcohol it would be an enormous challenge and take a great deal of their own courage to change their drinking habits."

S.H. "Today is a really miserable day, weather wise. It is the middle of January, it is grey and raining outside and it seems a bit of an effort to feel joyful. I am sure lots of people in my part of the world feel that at the moment. Not to mention what is going on in our world right now. What words of 'encouragement' can you give me? I have just noticed my own use of the disguised word 'courage' in my own question here!"

H.S. "Yes, right. The word courage does not always mean a requirement for change. However, here I would suggest a change of mental state to a more positive one by opening to love. When you do that naturally a change of mental state will arise. Do it now and you will feel it my son."

S.H. "Yes, I have just done it. You are right I feel much more positive and more energised. I think the trick is to keep remembering to open up your heart when things seem a bit dour or miserable."

H.S. "Yes my son, always do this at such times and it will help all, enormously if they do. It is such a simple practise which can, not only change lives but also the world itself, literally."

S.H. "I can feel here as I sit writing these words of our conversation and with my heart more open, that this place, where I sit and write each day (a hotel in my home town), is an establishment where the staff are cared for by the management and owner of the business. It comes through into the fabric of the building. It, and they are loved. I feel that and being in such surroundings is part of why I feel comfortable sat in this place and to help me write these words."

H.S. "You are quite right to pick up on these things my son. That is quite true and you through your own presence in the moment sat here writing your words here are adding to the vibration."

S.H. "I feel it is healing for me certainly."

H.S. "Yes, it is for as we said previously you are more fulfilled completing part of your own destiny which is at last, the starting to write this book. Remember you will have up and down days. Like yesterday, you will write little and on other days a lot. It does not matter at all, how much or little you write each day. The main thing is that you write something and keep the flow continuing you see."

S.H. "Yes I do, thank you. In a way, I now feel like my whole life up until now, has kind of been a preparation so that I could write this book. Though, I also know it is not of course!"

H.S. "Yes, my son. In some ways it has been, you are quite right. Each person's life, is if you like, a preparation of their own soul towards awakening. A spiritual maturity if you like. However, this cannot come without living in love, not another but loving your own self.

The meaning of this is not exactly being in love with your own self. But feeling love within yourself, ideally also for yourself and certainly for all others wherever and whenever you are able."

S.H. "When will the world change into the world that I dream about. One where everyone is loving and kind to everyone else. When there is true peace in the world?"

H.S. "When everyone else wants it as much as you do my son."

S.H. "Yes, but when will that be. It makes me a bit angry that so many people are running countries, who I feel are very lacking in compassion and spiritual wisdom if you like and it scares me sometimes."

H.S. "My son, please let go and trust in the divine. All is as it should be at this point in time. Let us use a simple analogy. Imagine life is a movie and you are half way through watching it. However, because you are disturbed by some of the content of the movie you want it to hurry up and end because you know it does have a happy ending. In your case in life you are wanting the movie to finish now at the happy ending. However, the film is part way through only, so you must just be patient. Try to enjoy the movie as much as you can. You have no other positive choice. Remember, also most importantly that life is just like a movie. It is real and yet it is not real."

S.H. "How do you mean life is not real?"

H.S. "Yes, because you are the director and everyone else is playing in your own movie. However, you do not know this, i.e. to the point that you are fully aware, that you are all of it and so is everyone else in the same situation. You are so much more than you think you are. As incredible as it sounds!"

S.H. "So, there are no limitations to who and what I am? Can you expand a bit on this please?"

H.S. "Yes, my son. When you were little, just a boy, everything seemed new and shiny. As you have aged, it is a case of, 'I have seen this all before'. Part of you switches off, nothing seems so new and shiny any more. Correct?"

S.H. "Yes."

H.S. "Well this is normal. It is because part of your consciousness switches off because so much is familiar. Then things are missed like you switch to autopilot, yes."

S.H. "Yes, I know exactly what you mean. Life can become a bit dull and monotonous at times."

H.S. "Indeed, but only if you let it. You must try to keep the mind alive and open. Trying new things is a good habit to get into. You like your routines, do you not? So, there is a greater tendency for you to feel this way than someone who prefers not to have a regular routine. They are more open to new experiences. This leads to more growth. Routines can easily lead to boredom and less expansion of the mind and consciousness my son. You like your routines primarily for their safety. They keep your anxiety levels to a minimum. Do they not?"

S.H. "Yes, that is true."

H.S. "However, the more you stretch yourself towards new experiences. The more your anxiety diminishes. Is that not so?"

S.H. "Yes, that is true. But what would be the best way to get out of routines sometimes?"

H.S. "By having new routine. Let's say one day a week you set aside time for a new experience. You can call it the new experience day. It would be most fulfilling to have this on a weekend or another time when your whole family is free to participate. Just doing something different. Something you don't usually do or to visit or walk somewhere different to your usual places."

S.H. "Thank you I will try to do this. But how will this help me to expand my mind?"

H.S. "Because it becomes more open and aware of the new experience. However small or simple the experience is, you see?"

S.H. "Yes, okay I see. Could this process of writing this book by this method of question and answer count as another way of expanding my consciousness?"

H.S. "Yes of course, you already know that."

S.H. "Yes, I guess that is obvious. I find the process of keeping my mind in gear, so to speak for this process to occur though, quite tiring."

H.S. "It is because you are having to focus and concentrate on a task that is not familiar to you. That is why in part. Also, because you are writing down these words long-hand, that also is tiring."

S.H. "Yes, it is but I would not be able to type fast enough if I was using my computer to write down these words.

Also, can you explain further how our consciousness is expanded by doing new things regularly?"

H.S. "This is because you are using different parts of the brain for certain experiences. When you use more of your brain literally, it helps to trigger memories in your soul of things you have done previously."

S.H. "Do you mean in previous lives? I do believe in reincarnation. I have had experiences in this life which have proved to me that reincarnation is a fact."

H.S. "Do you want to expand on your experience here my son, for the reader's sake?"

S.H. "Okay. About eighteen years ago, I met someone. A woman at a meeting in a large house. We all had a meditation together in a large room. I had never met this woman before. She was sitting next to me. After a short time, I felt a very strong feeling of love for this woman. The feeling emanated extremely strongly from my chest and I felt it go to her. I knew straight away that there was a strong connection between us both. Later, that day I spoke to her about this feeling I had felt. I asked her if we could sit quietly in a room together and that I could ask questions, as we are doing now. I told her that I would be told about the reason for this connection. We did this and I was told by 'spirit' that we had been together previously as a couple. I had died young and that we had both been deeply in love. Once I had received this information as to why I felt this connection with her the strong sense of love which I felt for her diminished straight away to a level which I was more at ease with. It was like a cord was cut between the two of us emotionally.

When I told the woman in question, she informed me that while I was sitting quietly opposite her, enquiring about the reasons for our connection, she was shown visions which she said mirrored some of the details of the life which I explained to her, after I had been told about the reasons for our connection.

For me this was my own concrete proof of the truth of the existence of life after death. I have ever since that deeply personal experience, been deeply grateful that I experienced it. I will never forget it. I might add that, she and I never did have a relationship. Needless to say, the actual full experience was far more profound than this summary, might suggest."

H.S. "My son, thank you for sharing this very personal experience here. Indeed, this meeting was a gift for you from spirit. It was something you asked for and you chose not to follow up on the opportunity for your own reasons. I can tell you now had you chosen to be with her, your life would have turned out very differently. But not necessarily for the better. It would just have been a different path with many different experiences, to what you have had to date, of course the same is true for everyone. You did not make the right choice or the wrong one. You simply made your own choice in this regard. Did you not my son."

S.H. "Yes, I guess so. I do not regret my choice here.
    Can you explain more about how reincarnation work's?"

H.S. "Simple. You are all eternal. You all have many lives. This occurs until the soul decides it no longer needs more to grow. The soul can choose to grow in other ways than just physical lifetimes."

S.H. "It can?"

H.S. "Of course. There is no limitation to the ways, consciousness or spirit, or soul, call it what you like can be expressed or experienced. Consciousness is expressed and experienced in a multitude of ways and forms too numerous to mention. When the soul is ready it moves on to experience deeper and more shared experience. This is where the soul joins with its own group soul to experience something on a grander scale if you like. This is where there is not a sense of individual identity, more of just an awareness of being but not in bodily form. But another sense of presence and being which is difficult to explain, because it is not an experience your soul has conscious memory of. It occurs when your awareness feels and knows that it is truly a part of and is everything in your experience. If you were to experience such in your usual human form it would be damaging for your own mind. This is because to use your own phraseology, that you would not be able to 'handle it'!"

S.H. "I was speaking to an acquaintance of mine yesterday. I happened to mention a bit about the process of how I am writing this book, partly because I knew he would understand. However, I did mention that I sometimes have my own doubts about the source of the information I receive and I wonder is it just coming from my own subconscious, rather than a 'higher-level', for want of a better phrase."

H.S. "My son, it is fine and understandable that you should doubt yourself.
Firstly, what should be said, is that if the information were to be correct and it is here. It would not matter, as regards to what the source of the information is. Again, to use the analogy of the ocean, it is still all coming from the same ocean. It is just that parts of the same ocean are more aware and awake than other parts. This is not meant literally, to re-iterate your point. The difference as has been said before, my son, is that you have been able to open a conduit or a connection with the source of this information."

S.H. "The source. But what exactly and where exactly is this source?"

H.S. "The source is all around you within and without. The source is 'all that is'. The life force of everything. The awareness and consciousness in and around everything. That is who you are. Who and what all are."

S.H. "Why is it so difficult most of the time to see, know and believe this, though?"

H.S. "Because the normal belief pattern of your society does not believe or encourage this way of thinking. To do so would empower society. The rulers of your societies want to disempower not empower individuals. The rulers of your societies and establishment's want to hold onto power and wealth for themselves and the limited few. However, there comes a point where the rising levels of consciousness will cause a flood and humanity will awaken, all together to these truths."

S.H. "When will that be?"

H.S. "When the time is right, but in the near future, my son."

S.H. "Talking of rising consciousness levels makes me think, of rising sea levels. There is a lot of talk in this book about comparing mass consciousness to an ocean of 'being'. Is there a connection between the rising temperature levels and rising consciousness levels?

I sometimes wonder if the main cause of global warming could be more to do with the sun giving out more heat perhaps, than burning fossil fuels?"

H.S. "My son, you would be correct. The sun is indeed heating up your Earth more. There is a reason why this is occurring. The sun is an intelligent being in its own right, which, will not surprise you! However, to most people it is just a big bright thing in your sky, be it keeping everything alive.

Now, remember like a sort of parent, it is keeping everything alive, for without it you would all perish from your physical existence.

To keep it simple for all to understand. The sun knows what it is doing to change the consciousness of your Earth and all that lives on it. The changes that this heating up will help to bring about will help to raise the consciousness of your world in many ways and for the better. This is why it is occurring at this time. Even if all your carbon emissions were to stop the Earth's temperature would continue to rise within controlled measure because of the consciousness, indeed 'loving intent' of your sun.

You see my son in the same way that the sun radiates, so do you my son and it is beautiful to behold. Along with a multitude of others of course."

S.H. "How will rising temperatures have a big effect on raising levels of human consciousness, though? Many might argue that that it can and will cause great suffering for so many."

H.S. "My son firstly, this is a slow process. So, people have time and chance to make changes in plenty of time. Even if this means moving locations. People on seeing the physical changes will inevitably make massive changes to their lives and beliefs for the better in a myriad of ways and for many reasons. This is a major factor in why in part a large shift in human consciousness will result and why if you like it will be a sort of gift from your sun. Which in truth is from 'God' as the sun of course is part of 'God'."

S.H. "I would love it if this planet was totally and utterly inhabited by only highly evolved human beings. The world I am sure would have to be a much better place then, for everyone to live."

H.S. "My son, this is indeed the destination of your planet. Though it will take a little time yet. In the grander scope of things, there is no rush. Though of course, most would think there is. But in the heart of 'all that is' there is no fear, only experience. For all your chosen experiences are being experienced by 'all that is' or 'God' if you like too. Remember these are just literal identities or labels placed on something beyond words."

S.H. "Blimey, thank you. What I love with some of these answers is the comfort the words bring me in lots of ways, including a form of verification to help melt away my doubt about the source of my answers."

H.S. "My son, as this process expands, with time the connection improves and the flow becomes more congruent and clearer."

S.H. "A big question now! Can you tell me a bit about the significance of the current period which humanity is in please?"

H.S. "My son, this is a time of transit, a time of change, a time of flux. There is a big shift in humanity's consciousness going on right now. It is a generational shift primarily. The consciousness held by the younger generations to your own, is quite different and you can feel it. The torch is in the process of being passed from one generation to another right now. All that is happening in politics, on the world stage, appears retrograde but it is not. This change will increase the speed to the new, as time will show. Before something new can be created, the old must be destroyed, or pulled down. You are living now, in the dismantling stage before the rebuild. It is alarming because no one is sure what will take the place of the old. Be reassured, the old will be replaced with a great improvement in forward thinking, though it does not seem so. Sometimes a flood is required to sweep away what needs to pass. Keep your faith my son and trust in the process, all is as it should be. Do not fear for the future. The future will take care of itself."

S.H. "Thank you. All I would say, is that the answer here seems a bit vague or non-specific."

H.S. "We cannot be more specific. The question is too open. As we have said it is a time of great change. It is a time when the consciousness of one generation is taking over from another and all that will follow will stem from this shift in consciousness. However, this will take time i.e. several years. It will not be overnight."

S.H. "Okay, I see. So, will these changes be reflective in a greater awakening in humanity to our true nature i.e. that we are all divine beings, connected and part of 'all that is', or 'God,' or whatever you want to call it?"

H.S. "Yes, that is true but to different degrees for everyone. Each flower opens when it is ready. You see nothing is forced. Free choice reigns supreme, as always. There is no other way."

S.H. "How can I take a part in this change. I like to think that although I am one of the baby-boomer generation, that I do indeed hold some of the characteristics, of the consciousness of this younger generation."

H.S. "You do, or you would not be wanting to be writing this book my son. It is because of this desire to be an agent of change in consciousness, that you do so much of what you do my son. You do know that in your heart. Keep shining your own light as you do. Even just by doing this you are fulfilling your main reason for being here now. All else that you do is an addition to this and you choose to do it. There is no pressure on you to do it. The only pressure you feel is the pressure that you put on your own self about the process of writing this book and all it entails. As you have been told already, just take it each day as it comes. Let this project unfold bit by bit and it will be made manifest. Trust in the process of life. Love will ensure the outcome."

S.H. "Someone I know, finds it difficult to 'open their heart' at will. They say they don't even understand what I mean. What is the best way to teach them what I mean by this and how to do it?"

H.S. "The way is through example firstly. This is about unconditional love partly. You can give them examples of what you mean, as you have already done so. The concept will confuse some. Firstly, the other person needs to understand that in the body, the heart is the seat from where you feel the love emanate. So, it passes through it. It is not generated by it. It is the heart 'chakra' that opens or closes as the heart is functioning. It seems simple to you my son, as you have mastered this process when you choose. Others have not. Keeping the heart chakra open is easy, once you know how. But for many there are emotional blockages which need releasing to enable them to complete the process so that love can flow freely. The best way to do this is to let go of emotional suffering and resentments of past hurts. To do this requires forgiveness firstly and through forgiveness of others followed by self-forgiveness, so these hurts can be released. However, the forgiveness needs to be deeply felt to enable the opening of this chakra. To forgive oneself means releasing judgements of oneself i.e. that one is a failure or not good enough or one's self is bad when it is not. To release these judgements nictitates a change of mind and attitude about oneself. An acceptance of who we are and what we are and trusting in ourselves, in our own inherent goodness. It is the self-judgement in a negative way that causes the blockages. Not how others feel about ourselves. But how we or the individual feel about ourselves."

S.H. "But how can someone most easily let go of this self-judgement, if it has been held onto for a long time?"

H.S. "It helps tremendously if the individual can see that their own negative self-judgement is the reason for their own toil and woe and hurt that they have inflicted on themselves. Even if it is judgement of another about action they took. It is still self-judgement about another that they can let go of through forgiveness.

Forgiveness is the key. For forgiveness is just another word for love and 'love is the key'. Love is the force and the power to 'open' your heart."

S.H. "Changing the subject. I feel that having stopped drinking alcohol will make me a purer and clearer channel to receive these words. Would I be correct in this assumption?"

H.S. "Yes, my son, you would. Alcohol blocks the process to some degree. It is not just the physical effects of alcohol but also the effect on the etheric body, for this is dulled by alcohol too."

S.H. "How is the etheric body affected by drinking alcohol?"

H.S. "Because it dulls your light and energy. When the physical body is weakened the energy of the etheric is diminished because one relies on the other, they are connected.

When a battery is low on power, say in a torch, it emits a weaker light. To use an analogy. The etheric body is not the spiritual body. The etheric is however, connected to spirit through the body. The spirit is the awareness, the etheric is part of the life force emitted from the physical body. When alcohol is consumed, the body is not functioning to its optimum level and the physical body is affected reducing the energy level latent in the body because the body functions are slowed down and suppressed including the emotions."

S.H. "One last question on the ability of the etheric body being affected indirectly via the physical body being affected by alcohol consumption. Is this because the etheric body acts a bit like an antenna so the signal is reduced such as in receiving these communications?"

H.S. "Yes, my son it is, to keep the process simple."

S.H. "As I write, my wife and I have stopped consuming alcohol entirely. How is this likely to affect our own emotional state and relationship?"

H.S. "Firstly my son. It will make your relationship more honest. More clear. More healthy. More sensitive to each other's needs and desire. You will be more in tune with each other. More receptive and better listeners to each other. Your communications and understanding of each other will improve. Need I say more?"

S.H. "No, not really. What I see is a reflection of the improvement in the individual's health and well-being, being mirrored in the relationship."

H.S. "Yes, honesty being the main one."

S.H. "We all get caught up in our own lives, don't we? I myself included. So often I feel and think that I am so self-consumed. Caught up in my own thoughts, feelings and fears. It makes me feel quite selfish. I look at others and see that most people are much the same. We are each the centre of our own little universes or worlds. It is as if our focus is almost entirely on ourselves, as if our awareness hardly ever strays from our own problems and concerns. I think this is the source of most of the problems in the world. Innate human selfishness. The worst part is I feel, I am just as bad as the rest when it comes to selfishness. My thoughts are always it seems, about myself."

H.S. "My son, are you sure? Do your own fears not revolve so often about the wellbeing of others you meet?"

S.H. "Yes, that is true."

H.S. "So, do not judge yourself so harshly my son. Your focus ultimately- a great deal of your time-revolves around others; including strangers. You do yourself a disservice here. So much of your time is spent reflecting on others, including family members. Your time right now, here writing, is being spent with a view to improve the lives of others and ultimately the state of the world. Is it not?

You have stopped drinking any alcohol at this time to improve the quality of your spiritual connection to the source of these words. Have you not?

Even if you are rightly aware of the benefit of this, to your own well-being, as well. This is all highly commendable. See in yourself, all the good you do. All the joy you create for others, as well as yourself. You are a much more thoughtful and considerate person towards others than you realise yourself to be my son!"

S.H. "Thank you for those dear and encouraging words. I feel that I needed to hear that said at this time. I don't feel down. Just that maybe I should be doing more."

H.S. "You are doing more than enough already my son. Even, each bit of cleaning you do at home is done for others, as much as it is for yourself. You forget this fact. Do you not?"

S.H. "Yes, I do."

H.S. "So even if it is just for your own family only, you are still doing them a service. You are doing it for others here too, no matter how routine it may feel. Your life involves a lot of self-sacrifice for others my son. This you also take for granted. In the sense that you forget so much of what you do, is for others as well as yourself. Even picking up a piece of litter!"

S.H. "Thank you."

S.H. "I feel I keep on getting drawn off target with this chapter. This book which I plan to call 'Awakening to Love'.

This chapter is about the process and meaning of awakening to our true 'essence', which is that we are really consciousness, or spirit.

I am writing this book long-hand in the first instance, before typing it onto my computer. When I have finished writing the book then each booklet which I have written, I am hoping will constitute a chapter in the finished article."

H.S. "Firstly my son, do not worry about being drawn off target, as you mention, for you are still getting used to this method of writing. It is still a little unfamiliar to write down the words you are receiving. Is it not?"

S.H. "Yes, it is indeed."

H.S. "Then secondly, the meaning of 'awakening to love' is just that. The use of the words here 'awakening to love', in the context of your meaning is correct at the deepest level of awakening as an individual. What in essence firstly, is love?

It is not just a feeling that humans feel within themselves or is projected by others. It is an example of love. But the true essence is completeness. This a completeness of understanding, of understanding life itself. The source of life is energy. But not energy that can be measured or seen or picked up. It is invisible to your eyes, yet it powers all around you and is the force that enables and gives life to all things. It pervades all of creation. In the physical world and the non-physical. So, it is the essence of what and who you truly are. This force is awareness itself. Because this is the essence of love it is best experienced through your feeling of it while in the human form. To do this means to open what you call, the heart chakra, which is an energy centre located level with your chest and heart. Through the vibration of love, you will experience your knowing oneness, at a level and vibration much higher and quicker than thought itself. You can know something in an instant. You receive information this way at a much higher rate, more quickly, more deeply, more comprehensively than through the brain 'mind', for it is much more effective at passing and receiving information, as it is your true way of knowing and accessing information. People access information like this all the time, but most do not understand how it gets to them, or where it comes from. They just assume it has arisen in their own minds.

The information that you are receiving now as you write, it is an aspect of this connection but is as if being translated from feelings into words. The words come from your own vocabulary. Yet you are being prompted as it were with the vibrations of knowingness which are being relayed. It is a bit like a painter being channeled with the idea for a painting and then painting it but only with the paints available in his pallet, you see?"

S.H. "Yes, I see."

H.S. "Then thirdly, you ask about the technical process of writing. It is best at this time, as you are learning the process of writing down these words, to do it in long-hand as it is in tune with the pace of the information supplied. Typing it directly would be too slow for the speed the words are received and 'translated' by your own mind. This as we previously described.

Then fourthly, we will endeavour to supply this information if you like so that each booklet you write into can be used congruently as a chapter in the book to come. We will give you the chapter name at the start of each book. Does this make it easier for you my son?"

S.H. "Yes, it does. Thank you. So, can we confirm that the title will be 'Awakening to Love'."

H.S. "Yes, my son."

S.H. "What about the title for the first chapter i.e. this first book I am handwriting"?

H.S. "How about, 'Love, what is it all about?'"

S.H. "Really?"

H.S. "Yes my son, really!"

S.H. "Okay. So, then that has cleared up a few more of my questions I think. So, moving on then. We have spoken a bit more about the essence of love at a deep level. I like to think I know this now. The trickier thing now that I find, is keeping my focus on this knowledge and keeping my heart open to love. I feel that part of me closing much more than it is open. My mind and physical emotions, such as fear and anxiety keep on getting in the way of love and compassion. I get annoyed with myself at such times. I am then aware of not feeling joyful. I am not open to feeling such love. It is frustrating."

H.S. "Of course it is my son. But do not be so hard on yourself. You have chosen to be incarnated in this place, in the body you are in to learn. To learn more about the experience of being in a human body."

S.H. "I have?"

H.S. "Yes, my son. Not just you, but everyone else too."

S.H. "Really."

H.S. "Yes, really. Why else would you be here?"

S.H. "I don't know, by accident maybe. Lots of people believe in a sort of chaos theory. That everything has happened by chance but according to the rules of science, that there is no God and everything we are talking about here is just nonsense."

H.S. "Indeed, my son but that is not truth. The truth is the reason they are here now is to learn the truth about how and why they are here. They have forgotten the very reason why they have turned up for the party."

S.H. "The party, what do you mean?
    Is that just a figure of speech?"

H.S. "No my son. Life if lived correctly, should be and can be a party if lived how God intended. To feel love and joy for all creation throughout your journey. You have free choice, all do. It is just that most people choose differently. They feel sadness and pain, due to their ignorance of their true nature and the joy I speak of simply evades their life experience. At least for most of it. Yet they have fleeting moments of this deep joy. But for most it remains elusive, for the vast majority of their lives. They need to simplify things. The simpler, the less complex their lives, then the more they can be in the moment. Just being, rather than doing. That is why you are called 'human beings' and not 'human doings'."

S.H. "I feel very fortunate in many ways with my life. Although I feel there have been great struggles at times for me, both mentally and physically. I know that this is nothing out of the ordinary. I know that this is the nature of life and that our experiences are opportunities for growth. What is the best way to maximise our growth from our more difficult and painful experiences?"

H.S. "Indeed the purpose of life is to learn and grow and ultimately to remember who you are. Your true nature and closeness to the spirit within you. The spirit within never leaves you, it has never left you or you it!
    It is the eternal essence of your true nature. It is who you truly are. In your dreams your spirit soars. It is your spirit that flies, when you often dream of flying. Your spirit is free to soar. Your consciousness creates all within your dreams. Your consciousness is co-creating

with God with spirit. This is the power of your consciousness. It is different to your mind."

S.H. "Now this is something I have never understood. Can you please explain the difference between the human mind and consciousness?"

H.S. "You are not your mind. But you are consciousness. Remember words are labels. By their nature, they are very limited as a means of describing things. We have perceptions about the meaning of words. Consciousness is unlimited. Mind is limited however. Your consciousness is not limited to your body. When the body dies so does the mind. Consciousness never dies, it is eternal. Mind is a shallow imitation of consciousness. Mind is like the reflection in the mirror of something. It is not real. Though that being reflected is real. The mind is powerful; however, it only exists because conscious awareness exists. You are not the mind. Thoughts are just like the clouds crossing the sky. They come and go. Consciousness to use a very simple analogy is like the sky permanent to you. Mind is like the clouds. Ephemeral. Thoughts come and go with less substance. Though still with a power to create. For they spring from your consciousness but are expressed through the mind."

S.H. "Is it possible to think thoughts outside the body where your mind does not exist?"

H.S. "Yes, my son but it is a different type of thinking. It is pure knowing at a higher level. It is a feeling type of experience rather than a thinking, as you experience it in your body. It is the same as how you dream. In dreams, you do not think. Thought is suspended and feeling and knowing take over."

S.H. "Thank you for explaining that. Could you please also now explain something else for the readers. I introduce each answer beginning with the initials H.S. I know that for me this means

'Higher-Self'. I already have my own understanding of this term. Can you explain what the 'Higher-Self' is?"

H.S. "My son, this is a soul related description. Firstly the 'soul' is the spiritual body within the physical body. The soul is not the physical. It leaves the body on death of the physical body and returns to the different dimension to which the soul resonates with most. When it does so it merges with other aspects of itself which are part of the field of consciousness. These other parts of the soul make up the group soul. The group soul is an amalgamation of all the lives on many different dimensions experienced by the group soul. The group soul is a part of 'all that is' but has its own identity at the same time. Just as you experience individuality in your own current experience. All co-exist at the same time. Higher-Self here, is reference to the energy of the group soul, to which you belong. It is difficult to explain something which infers separation, when in truth none exists. At the highest level, it is a bit like asking, when you are told you are part of the ocean, yet really the ocean. You ask, which part of the ocean am I?

Though equally to still use the same analogy you are part of the ocean but also the whole ocean. It is the same as if your human identity and mind having been told you are just a tiny part of the ocean and keeping your focus always pointed on that one aspect of limitation. People are like the fish swimming in the ocean (using the same analogy for God) and asking, 'where is this ocean I keep hearing about'?"

S.H. "Yes, I do like the analogy of the fish in the ocean, asking where is the ocean.

So, all this information is coming from the ocean of consciousness around me which I am also simultaneously, around me.

So, on one level it comes from me. But at the same time, it comes from what everyone else is a part of too?"

H.S. "Yes, my son. That is true. All of creation can in theory, access this information through their inner knowing. Even plants and rocks experience inner knowing. They have consciousness too. In the same way the earth's ocean too, is an entity with inner knowing. The body of the earth has inner knowing. As does the sun and all suns in the universe. In fact, suns or stars are sources of tremendous wisdom, which is why they have the ability to hold the fate and destiny of world's such as your planet."

S.H. "So, one day could I evolve and become the consciousness of a sun somewhere in the universe and control a whole solar system."

H.S. "Yes, my son, you could. However, it would not be the individual you, but the greater aspect of your being to which your soul belongs. It is an energetic thing rather than a bodily thing. There are no words in your language to describe such. This is because there are no human experiences to measure such evolvement to. It is evolvement at a very high level. It is pure love. The light emitted from your sun is 'pure love'. Light is love. Scientists cannot explain what light is truly. But it is pure love. Love is integral to consciousness."

S.H. "Maybe that is part of my greater, far off destiny. Maybe everybody's, who knows. You call me my 'son' often enough, ha-ha?"

H.S. "Yes, indeed."

S.H. "What is heaven or the next world like, the place we go to when we die?"

H.S. "Firstly, let's say it will feel to you and your senses very much like this world. It is a place between worlds, as there are many stages of progression for the spirit or consciousness. As Jesus said, 'there are many mansions in my father's house'. You could call these stages or levels of spiritual progression. Dependant on the soul's degree of evolvement and mental state, it will depend on the nature of you when you first find yourself in the next world and dependant on your own karma or actions you took in your last life. The main difference you will find is that you will quickly learn that the mind creates your reality instantly in the spirit world where as in the human experience this does happen but at a much slower rate. You create your own reality in both fields of experience because consciousness is indeed the builder. I will give you an example, on the earth plane, say you are looking for a new job. You are not happy with your current job. You look around and make enquiries to find another one. Correct?"

S.H. "Yes, that is the normal thing to do."

H.S. "You do not in most cases wait for a job to find you, do you."

S.H. "No because you could be waiting a very long time if you did."

H.S. "Indeed my son. But if you waited long enough someone would at some point offer you a job doing something even if you did not really want one. Correct?"

S.H. "Yes, probably."

H.S. "The reason for this is because the universe is aware that a job would be to your advantage. It knows your needs. You do not have to put out what you need, it will come to you anyway. However, if you use your mind and actions to bring about a new job more quickly, this can also happen. Correct."

S.H. "Yes. The point being?"

H.S. "The point being simply, you are looked after whether you are aware that you are or not. In the spirit world, this process happens also but instantly my son. That is the main difference. It happens instantly because everything is controlled by your consciousness and not by physical laws as in your current world."

S.H. "So it is correct to say that there has never been a time that any of us have not existed?"

H.S. "Yes my son. But not the individual you. The personality comes and goes like the body. In the same way as some experiences in your mind live on, so will the individual as a memory but not the individual. The individual, is an aspect of the soul's consciousness but not the soul. Each lifetime you experience is 'logged' so to speak as an aspect of that consciousness and each soul and group soul, are in turn recorded as aspects of 'all that is' at the highest level of consciousness of which all are part of yet unaware of at the normal conscious level. To become aware of it, requires a total letting go and immersion to the highest vibration. To try to describe such, is very difficult, based on the limitation and definition of your words of your language. It is like the droplet letting go of its consciousness that it is a droplet when placed in the ocean. It becomes the ocean if it lets go to the idea it is now part of the ocean. You as 'perceived' human individuals refuse to let go to that idea, as you feel separate, yet you are always surrounded and immersed in this ocean of entirety."

S.H. "Thank you. So, we all exist in this ocean of conscious awareness, most us thinking we are separate from the rest. Isolated and alone. With the idea and belief that to feel loved that we need another to give us love. Forgetting all the time that we are love. We are loved and that we ourselves are the source of the very love, most of us yearn for."

H.S. "Yes my son, quite correct. The vast majority of your species are living in the dark, with your eyes shut, groping for the answers to life. All you need to do is open up, to the inherent wisdom of your own souls, which are directly connected to this ocean of love and wisdom. This being your true and real essence. The birth right of you all. However, your society and experiences are in denial of this truth, perpetuating and keeping alive the idea that you are separate and vulnerable."

S.H. "This in turn then perpetuates the idea of lack and keeps fear alive. It divides society and sets us against the other. It is sad. I just wish more could be more open or wake up to our true inheritance i.e. that we are all part of 'God', the ocean of love and awareness that we all share.

I feel that in the West especially there is a spiritual famine and so many people are suffering from it. That so many of our problems stem from this lack of understanding."

H.S. "Yes, my son. But things are improving. You may not see it but many are waking up to a higher consciousness. This is reflected in part by a sea of protest on your planet towards the ideas and instructions of certain politicians. Your social media is a physical reflection of this greater awareness. The social media has been born in part out of this higher awareness. For it is an interconnectedness of things physical inspired by this higher consciousness. The internet being inspired in those by this higher consciousness which in turn is helping to wake you up to all that is occurring on your planet.

Things are happening right now as all are observing, at great speed. This is partly due to the internet but also because of the increased 'vibration' on your planet.

This increased 'vibration' of which we speak is an aspect of this higher consciousness of all. As the vibration raises which is an outpouring of love from the 'God-head', so the consciousness of all will raise. Society is now very close to a bursting point, to an even greater degree of raised consciousness. It is the point of birth of a new higher consciousness for humanity. Until now it has been the 'gestation' period but the birthing is now proceeding. This is why there is such great upheaval and speed of occurrences. Ride this wave with peace and calm my son as much as you are able. You are doing what is right for you. Trust that others, 'all' others are doing what is right for them. All have a part or role to play in the drama. By drama we do not mean to belittle what is occurring. It is, that as real as it seems, it is a momentary drama to those watching on as most of society are caught up in the drama not realising the greater truths previously described to you about your true nature and the erroneous believe of much of humanity, that they exist separate from the rest of nature. Therefore, we use the term 'drama'."

S.H. "Thank you. It helps to hear that everyone is fulfilling a role no matter how precarious our world feels right now. I think a lot of older more mature people are pretty frightened."

H.S. "Yes my son. Do not be afraid. Remember there is no death. It is the lingering idea of death that frightens you all the most. There is no death. Only transition to another form. Love will conquer all perceived foes my son. Trust in the process of what is occurring now my son. Let go of your fears. Try as much as you can to convey peace and harmony to those around you.

My son, you have all chosen to be here at this time of great upheaval and transition. It is a time of great opportunity for the growth of your souls awakening. This is why so many souls have incarnated at this time. Partly for the opportunity for growth and partly to play your own roles in easing the transition from this epoch to another. From a time of darkness to a time of light. The light will prevail my son."

S.H. "I seem to find the questions i.e. coming up with relevant, interesting questions harder during the course of this process than I do with the answers. The answers simply flow back to me. I wish the questions would flow easier too. Any advice on this score?"

H.S. "My son it is funny, is it not that the scope for questions is almost unlimited unlike the answers. Yet the questions are the most challenging. What we might suggest is to feel for the questions rather than think <u>for</u> them. Let the questions arise from a feeling rather than a conscious mental process."

S.H. "Okay, I will. The idea for writing a book arose in part because of a message my sister passed on to me many years ago. A psychic she visited happened to mention to her, that one day, I would be a successful writer. I have never forgotten that. So, part of my reason for writing this book, is this positive message I received."

H.S. "Indeed my son. If she told you that you would be an unsuccessful writer you would probably never have tried to be one. Words of encouragement are very powerful are they not. Those words despite being received long ago, have helped shape your life. To the point, you are here now writing this. However, those words were but a spark which ignited the fire which now rages within you and brings these words so elegantly to these pages. We praise you for this as we help to guide your hand in the process."

S.H. "Thank you. Please tell me what does the world and the people of the world need to hear the most now to help restore peace in the hearts of those individuals and nations in conflict?"

H.S. "Such individuals need to follow their own inner guidance my son. They need to follow their own inner wisdom which all possess. This is the birth right of all. Instead, in the cacophony of noise that surrounds so many of your societies there is too much interruption to give peace sufficient chance to allow one's intuition to take the lead. People are so caught up in the pace of their lives and its many irrelevant distractions to give peace a chance. People must learn to give peace a chance to help them to access more of this inner learning. The source of true wisdom. This does not apply to all people by any means, my son, but it does apply especially to those in power. Those are the people who most need to make and be led by their inner 'teacher'. All your electronic devices tell you about the moment at hand. However, they distract you from the moment at hand and keep you in the dark. You see my son, when you are in the 'present' you are in the presence of God and the benefit of that is, your mind is still and love has a chance to make itself known to you. Contained within the love inherent in peace lays the guidance you all seek at any given moment. But you must surrender to it, to be in it and connected to it."

S.H. "I believe that too. The trouble seems to be, most people just don't believe that. They believe overall that their own mind is the master and the only guiding light in their own lives. That is why I think, so many are self-obsessed and prone to selfish thinking. It is as if most people are just focused only on their own lives and ignore the rest. This to me is the source of so much that is wrong in the world right now."

H.S. "Yes, you are right my son. This book is a part of trying to change that. To help shift the thinking of some people to the greater whole rather than just themselves. You are talking here of 'inclusive expansion' rather than 'selfish isolation'. This is reflected through what is going on right now in parts of your world. This is coming to the surface for all to see, clearer than ever. It is forcing many to look at their own conscience more closely. This is no coincidence my son. It is so timely. The very thing which needs to be addressed is the lesson of the day. This is no coincidence that it is happening now. In this respect, the uprising of protest towards ideas which are short of the target i.e. not right, are in turn becoming targets. In this respect, your social media is of great benefit to spread this positive uprising of human consciousness. For have no doubt. This is the ocean of rising consciousness of those more evolved, against those who hold onto views which belong to a different era. This protest will help a great deal to extinguish such prejudice to make such views obsolete, a thing of the past."

S.H. "It is great to see people power. For so long the people, the masses in so many civilised countries have felt an apathy due to a sense of powerlessness. These protests towards elected leaders wrong doing is showing that people do have power. A lot of power to hopefully change things for the better."

H.S. "Yes, my son. Part of the message here however, is that even those leaders causing the protest have a useful purpose in bringing out and being the reason for protest. They are only there due to the consciousness of those people who elected them.

However, even those who elected such people will see what occurs and change their own minds about things because of their choices and actions."

S.H. "We are talking about Donald Trump here and what is happening in the world right now. His inauguration was a week ago (as I write) and there have already been many protests due to his actions so far. I hope when he is replaced that the USA have learnt one lesson and have much more stringent methods about the suitability of candidates before they even stand for election. I would love to see only highly evolved, spiritual human beings elected to such high roles. We need this for many reasons. Not just to ensure peace prevails."

H.S. "Yes, my son. This can only occur when there is a sufficiently high enough consciousness for humanity as a whole. The leader reflects the consciousness in question. Each country is different. Each soul chooses which country in which to incarnate, before they are born. Not according to their own conscience but dependent on a variety of factors. Sometimes it is a high calling to bring positive change to a country. This is not the case with Donald Trump but for many it is the case. At the time of birth, they will find themselves in a country and in a time period which most resonates with them you see."

S.H. "Yes, I understand that. There are many sub-questions we could go off into about different time frames. You allude to the idea of choosing time frames to incarnate into rather than just a linear one."

H.S. "Yes, my son. There are many worlds within worlds. Many worlds, you incarnate into one of them. In the same way as you choose one family, one mother, one country. There are many choices for the soul to make."

S.H. "I don't really want to get into complicated ideas here. I feel that there is a benefit to keeping the questions and answers simple and easy to understand for most people. Including young people."

H.S. "Indeed my son. This is your choice it is all up for discussion if you so choose."

S.H. "Yes, I know, thank you. Moving on then. How can somebody, anybody most easily awaken to the spirit or soul within?"

H.S. "My son. Good question! The answer is simple.
Ask. Ask the spirit within to show itself. To reveal itself. To express itself, each and every day. To bring to the surface the divine gifts inherent in each individual.

When expressing the gifts within, the most joy will be experienced by each individual and the connection with spirit will be felt and experienced in the moment how divinity itself intended for that individual to express and be in the world.

The paradox is that you are all human beings too busy to be such, as most are 'human doings'!

Busy doing so much, forgetting just to be present in the moment, unless you are doing that which expresses the spirit. But here I am talking about doing that which keeps you from expressing the spirit. Even if it is just worrying about the next moment in front of you. Whatever the reason for why you are not at peace. When you are not at peace, you are not fully in the moment. You are not in the presence of God."

S.H. "Do you mean not 'fully' in the presence of God. Surely if you are simply alive, you are in the presence of God to some degree?"

H.S. "Yes, that is true. We are talking here about 'truly present'. As we were discussing earlier (not included in the book) there were times when you struggled and you now realise how distant you were from the present moment because of your worries and your fears. Your mind felt total disconnection from your spirit, from your soul, from peace and from the divinity within you. It was totally hidden from yourself for various reasons. Now when you reflect on that time in your own words, you remember how difficult it was and you see how far you have come in so many ways. This is due to your healing of yourself and in turn raising your own consciousness. Is that not so my son?"

S.H. "Yes, it is. My meditations have helped tremendously with healing myself. I have often said it is the best thing I have ever learnt to do."

H.S. "Yes, my son. It has been so good for you. It is also such a good practice for anyone who takes the time to practice it, be it you, or whoever making the connection with the divine inherent within <u>all</u>. To do so there must be a preparation to face one's fears and worries. These will come up into the forefront of one's consciousness until they are healed. But that is why they keep coming up in the mind. Once they are healed, the thoughts and ideas in question will stop arising to be faced. It is a most worthy practice and one that cannot be practiced enough."

S.H. "How much can refining our diet to a healthy one, such as reducing our intake of foods like sugar, saturated fats and the like improve our strength and spiritual connection. Are we then purer and more connected to the spirit world?"

H.S. "Yes, you are more connected due to greater strength and health of the body. This is no surprise my son. But equally important as you have experienced is to purify the mind and heart of negative thoughts and emotions. Whether they be about oneself or others. Both are equally damaging to the individual."

S.H. "What is the best way to release and heal ourselves of these negative thoughts and emotions?"

H.S. "Again ask the divine for help with these emotions. Practice self-forgiveness. Operate from an open heart. Be selfless and serve others wherever you can. Love all. Serve all."

S.H. "Surely though this is difficult when sometimes others are horrible to us."

H.S. "Yes my son, but the only way they will change is if they are treated with love. Unconditional love is the best way to teach them the way."

S.H. "I have had an interesting last twenty-four hours, emotionally. So, I am keen to get down on paper, some of what has come to me.

This is related in to what this book is all about which is 'Awakening to Love'.

On paper most people, I think would understand the premise of this book's title. However, they would I think struggle to write a book about it. This is not me blowing my own 'trumpet' so to speak. Just how could you write a whole book about it?

Anyway, we have spoken a bit about the true essence of love. But how do we awaken to it?

How do we awaken to something which most of us know exists? The trouble is most of us look to get this love from others. Most people I think, or at least a great many think you can't get it for yourself from yourself. It must be given to you by someone else.

The reason for this in part, I think, is because so many people are walking around with so much pain that there is no room inside themselves, to feel love for themselves."

H.S. "Yes, my son that is so. Carry on, you want to say more on this subject."

S.H. "Yes, I do. I've been watching a programme on television. A reality show for the whole of the last month. I like watching people and I am interested to see what I can learn about other people's behaviour. The main thing which struck me about the programme was how little I learnt about the people featured in it!

One of the people who had been in the month-long series. Soon after was in a different programme which focused on helping this individual with his issues and problems. The point of all this is that it turned out that this person needed to learn also, to love himself more.

He was sent away by a counsellor having been told to do this. The individual agreed this would be a good thing to do and off he went. But, the point I am trying to make here is that he was not shown or told as far as I could tell how he could 'love himself' more, so that he could heal some or all his emotional pain.

Most of us suffer similar pain, either some of the time or most of the time. Few people, would I say, never feel no emotional pain if any.

We have already talked about existing, at the deepest level as an ocean of consciousness, which is omniscient, omnipresent and omnipotent and that we are divine love. That we are loved and we are also the source of that love.

But, we must first, if it feels right, and that this is true, embrace this idea fully. Once we have fully accepted this belief and come to know its truth, then and only then, can we embrace it, within ourselves.

A good example of this is the following analogy imagining the ocean to be the love which surrounds us.

Imagine that you are an egg-timer full of sand. The top of the egg-timer is level with the ocean's surface. The surface is still and calm. Imagine the sand slowly draining out. As it does so, the sand is replaced by the water. Or the love that we are. Which surrounds us and is always accessible. As our pain is released, instead we are feeling filled with love. We need to learn to do this naturally as we go about our day. With practice and time, it can become simple.

To learn a practice such as meditation, will make this practice more simple and natural.

There are of course many other ways through which we can teach ourselves to love ourselves more. At the deepest level, however. This is what I believe it means."

H.S. "Yes, indeed my son. You have explained it well here. However, the practice of using the egg-timer will be confusing and difficult for someone to understand, who has not meditated before. This is something that is familiar to you. For those who have never meditated there is a simpler method, which is this: -

The individual should look at themselves in a mirror as if they were looking at another person, whom they had never met before. Though, at the same time they are aware of all their issues, worries and problems. In their mind, say to the reflection, 'I forgive you for all that you have done to others which may have caused them hurt or pain. I also, forgive myself, for all the hurt and pain that I have caused to myself.'

Practice this each day for a week. Each time it is done observe the feeling and emotions that arise. Don't analyse them. Whatever comes up just let it go. Try not to think about it. This is a type of self-cleansing or healing process. This will enable the self-love to flow more easily through and to you, or whoever it is that practices this exercise."

S.H. "Thank you for that. Yes, we look so often to others for the love we crave. Other people can and do love us at times. Often though the amount of love they can give is never enough. We can feel like we need love to be drip fed to us. But to put that on another is not practicable, not sustainable and unfair.

Also, most of those people who feel they have that emotional burden are probably struggling to feel love themselves."

H.S. "Exactly my son. That is so true. We project onto others our feelings and needs and expect them to supply it. Humanity needs to learn that they are self-sufficient in love. It is natural to seek the affection of others but it is not essential to survive as all the love you crave is accessible within. When you know this, there is freedom from these emotional pains. You can release and let them go more easily to the embrace of the divinity inherent within you. Within you all."

four

A New Path

S.H. "My wife and I have given up drinking any alcohol, as I write. We are both moving towards a vegan diet, although I still eat fish. We both feel much better for making this change in our life style. I know that if we ensure we both stick to a balanced healthy diet, this should improve our own health.

But I am also interested in the 'spiritual' effect of such a diet on the individual. Can you please enlighten me further, regards this change in life style?"

H.S. "My son, welcome back to our conversations.

A vegan diet will be of great benefit to both of you. Drinking no alcohol, will also be of great benefit.

Alcohol not only dulls the physical senses but also the spiritual senses. These being in your case a variety of spiritual gifts. You have developed these abilities during your many lifetimes, including not least, in this one. However, my son, a diet rich in meat, dairy products and drugs including alcohol are not only detrimental to the physical health but also the mental health of humans. The connection with the divine, within you all, is temporarily broken at such times. The etheric body is less energised. We will give you an analogy; When a light emits a dull light, it is less visible to a moth and it will not see it, unless it is close to the light. When a light shines brightly, many moths will come to it. In the same way with human's, others will be drawn to a bright light shining from within the individual, as they sense something special within those individuals, with such a bright light. The reason the light is brighter is because their connection with spirit is stronger. It is stronger because the body is functioning at the optimum. Just as it does with a child in good health. There will be a greater purity and clarity of the individual accessing such a diet and regime and staying off drugs and alcohol.

The etheric body is stronger, more vibrant and has a stronger etheric connection to the subtler vibrations surrounding them. Like a more sensitive antenna, the reception will always be closer to the optimum which they are capable of receiving. The psychic and healing abilities of the individual will be greatly improved, allowing greater service to be rendered in such areas, including the method of writing you are conducting now my son."

S.H. "Thank you. This is as I thought. I am not surprised to hear this answer. It is however, hard sometimes to stick to a pure and healthy diet."

H.S. "Yes, my son. Self-discipline is called for. However, the benefits are well worth the effort. Don't you think so?"

S.H. "Yes, I certainly do. It also gets easier as time goes by. It does set you apart from others, from a social aspect however, i.e. it is harder going to places such as the pub, for obvious reason. However, I am determined to continue on my path."

H.S. "My son this is indeed the path for you. The best one and your calling. It is your way of helping others heal themselves. Just as you have had to learn to heal yourself."

S.H. "Yes, I think so. I am glad that I have the determination. I know many people struggle to find this in themselves. I hope these words help to inspire others, who are also trying to follow this path."

H.S. "My son as the body ages, there are many changes that occur within it. The body does not function as well as when you are young. You should take greater care of it. Similar, when the individual is a baby and the body is also fragile. This is similar but a reverse process. The body metabolises nutrients less efficiently. Some are required in a greater quantity, such as protein to maintain muscle. You should all listen to your own bodies. They have the inherent wisdom to indicate what is required by your intuitive promptings. These of course will also be more detectable the greater your sensitivity is to your own intuition. This is your inner guide or teacher. You are prompted however in the right direction with such things if you learn to recognise the signs when they appear within you."

S.H. "You mention 'intuition'. The inner teacher. I am also interested in what exactly the conscience is and how it compares with intuition?"

H.S. "My son, they are one and the same. They are the inner knowing which you all possess. If you would all but listen more often. So often and sadly, it is ignored by so many. They do not want the inconvenience of following a higher more compassionate route in life. This is often down to selfishness or a lack of awareness and the cause of much suffering in your world."

S.H. "The world is full of many temptations or choices each day. These can take us off the path if we let them. I suggest if we let our 'conscience' or 'higher knowing' guide us then we are most likely to stay on the path that the divine has chosen for us. Also, I suspect that path is the one which will lead to the most happiness and fulfilment. Not just for ourselves but for others as well."

H.S. "Yes, indeed my son. That is one of life's challenges. To stay on your own true path. That is true for you all and indeed it is a major part of the life experience. It is about learning to master the emotions rather than allowing the emotions to be the master of you. This begins with the mind. The individual needs to learn the power of the mind. To make your mind a friend and not a foe. This involves teaching yourself mindfulness. This means learning to be present in each moment. When you are not present in the moment, then you will not be aware of what thoughts are circulating in your own mind. People need to learn that mind is the builder. It has the power to create and shape lives and therefore the future. So, the mind needs to be used wisely in its focus for what you believe, so in time that on which you focus will become realised."

S.H. "These are profound words. What we focus on becomes our experience at some point."

H.S. "Yes, indeed my son. Keep your focus and your intentions pure. Keep them on your tasks at hand. Let your goals and focus remain on others and their happiness. This is because ultimately this will be to the benefit of your own happiness because as you have already had explained, you are all connected. Ultimately what you do to, or for another, you do to and for yourself. This will bring to you and all those who practice such the greatest peace and in turn joy.

Joy will help others awaken to who they truly are. You cannot feel true love without joy and you cannot feel true joy without love. They both walk hand in hand JOY=LOVE!"

S.H. "Can you tell me a bit more about the meaning of this chapter being titled 'A New Path'."

H.S. "Not only are you and your family on a new path of sorts now. So is the world of humanity. There is a great shift in progress. This is a shift of human consciousness. Human consciousness never stays still. Believe it or not all that is learnt by any human being who has ever lived is added to the great pool of consciousness that exists. Some might call it the mind of 'God' or simply 'all that is' of which you are all a part.

You will often see a synchronicity of thought and idea's in your communities, large or small whereby many have the same thought or idea. This is a consequence of the higher mind which connects you all. You could say that the synchronicity of thought of the global mind is now more connected and that this is because of the internet and social media. It is much easier to connect and be connected on a physical level. This however, also and not surprisingly affects the subconscious level of human consciousness and the speed of this interconnection. This means that change of many sorts will become quicker and quicker. I am sure you feel this as do many right now, about the speed of change in your world. It is now almost impossible to hide things from the people which once was easier for your politicians, the establishment and persons holding power over others. It is easier to protest and arrange protest towards ideas which do not resonate with the new consciousness. This is being carried now not surprisingly largely, by the younger generations, who are fulfilling their own destinies and purpose for incarnating at this time of fast change.

Fear, was the favourite tool of those in power to suppress the people. This is much more difficult now for the aforementioned reasons. The younger generations are more easily able to see through the methodology of using fear to suppress the older generations who have been indoctrinated, due to its hold over them. The changes the world is now set upon will come from the young not the old, as was previously always the case. This is because the power is now in the hands of the young. Not the old. This is because of your digital media and its speed and interconnectivity."

S.H. "I do worry a bit about the amount of fear I see though being propagated by the press and media about current political events.

This only makes many more anxious in an age when there is already so much stress and anxiety around. Anxiety being part of my nature, means I am very aware of its causes and try to limit my exposure to it to avoid its negative effects."

H.S. "This is true my son. It makes people feel vulnerable and powerless. But this power is often created by those in power for a reason. To have power over others and to influence how people think for their own ends. However, because of social media being so readily available, people cannot be controlled anywhere near as easily as they once could be. Now people can rise up and protest to prevent changes with which society do not agree. This is good. It will make it difficult for despots or dictators to succeed where they once could.

The main purpose of your book my son is to enhance the awareness of the interconnectivity of the human spirit-consciousness and what this means, how it works and its reality in truth.

This comes from encouraging others to go within their own selves and to look for their own answers to their own questions. If these words resonate with them so be it. If they do not, fine, then they should move on and find what does resonate in their own hearts and souls. There are many paths which lead to the truth. This chapter is helping to point to and define a new path in terms of the history of your planet. It is the digital age which is playing a large part in the social conscience of society."

S.H. "The social conscience of society. That is a new term to me."

H.S. "My son the definition is; a shared conscience of many. Whereby the thinking is largely the same, as are the beliefs and opinions held. With agreement resonating between the many, rather than discord being the result."

S.H. "Thank you. So, it sounds that in so many ways the world is in the safe hands of the masses. Rather than the dangerous hands of a few?"

H.S. "Yes, my son. At the highest levels of choice and freedom, love will always prevail, because love is the life force."

S.H. "The current zeitgeist is 'mindfulness'. I suppose this is an example which one could use, to demonstrate as an example of the truth about the existence of a group mind or consciousness of humanity. When lots of people pick up on something at the same time. Of course, this has happened with lots of smaller things. I think it is great though, that more people are being drawn to and becoming interested in topics like mindfulness."

H.S. "Yes, indeed my son. The irony or the paradox is it is called mindfulness and yet it is in part about keeping the mind clear to be aware of the present moment. So, it could easily have been called mind<u>less</u>ness. Yet this would indicate being in a semi-sleep state.

The concept or idea, has arisen largely as a means or type of coping strategy to survive in this modern very stressful world. Many people are trying to do too much too quickly. They are missing out on the world around themselves. They are sleep walking through their days. There are so many distractions to what is important which keeps them too busy to notice the beauty around themselves.

Tasks and employment need to be addressed of course. Yet the analogy of being on a hamster's wheel is true for many. The true purpose of life is not to work to earn money to live. Although this is how so many are brought up to think. The true purpose is to feel and express joy for themselves and others. To serve others wherever possible and to honour the planet on which you live. This means looking after it in a better fashion to which it is being treated currently. To preserve it for future generations as well as your own."

S.H. "What are the main things which humanity is doing to our planet which still needs to be addressed?"

H.S. "The planet Earth is a living breathing entity. Most are unaware that this is the case. The planet has its own mind or consciousness. In the same way, the ocean possesses consciousness. It is aware it is an ocean. In the same way, a red blood cell has its own consciousness and knows it is a red blood cell. A white blood cell knows it is a white blood cell. The Earth knows it is the Earth. The Earth does what it does for all creatures which exist upon it out of love. In the same way, the red blood cell does what it does out of love for the body. You do not direct the blood cells to do what they do. They know. The ocean or the Earth's crust do not do what they do out of chaos. They know what they do. When the sea is at storm, it knows. When a volcano erupts, it knows. There is a reason a logic behind it all.

The consciousness of humanity even influences what happens physically on your earth. The consciousness of humanity can even at times influence your weather patterns on extreme occasions. As you well know the weather also has a very strong effect on your own consciousness i.e. when the sun shines brightly, more likely you too will also radiate more joy. This is your own inner light being reflected not just to others, but to the sun also. The sun is even aware of your joy. As hard to believe by most, as it might be."

S.H. "Thank you."

S.H. "This morning I was reflecting during my meditation on some of my own inner struggles connected to my thoughts about certain others. I realise some of the characteristic's I find most difficult in some other people, are the very facets of my own character which I also have. One of these concern my own self-worth. How I judge my own success or failure relative to that of others. I find it difficult if I sense some degree of rejection by them. That can be quite challenging."

H.S. "Yes, my son that is because you feel unloved. That part of you deep, deep down inside your being is vulnerable to any form of rejection. Your tendency is to take this personally and see it reflected as a lack on your part. However, this is more often down to the judgement of others rather than your own about <u>self</u>.

Your judgement about others is being based on your own self-judgement. What you think about yourself you reflect onto others. You judge them in the same way you judge yourself. However, everyone judges in a slightly different way. Just because you feel one way about a certain individual does no more mean they judge you in the same way. Their judgements will be based on their own experiences. Though it is correct to say people do often project the character traits they don't like in themselves onto others."

S.H. "So, if we project our issues often onto others, then we have an opportunity to see them clearly through another, the more we can recognise that opportunity.

But, how do we know when it is a reflection of our own issues and not the other persons. How can we most easily distinguish between the two?"

H.S. "By how whatever it is, makes you feel. If you feel hurt rather than angry, it is most likely their issue. If you feel angry it can sometimes be your own. The best answer to this question is to go within and ask. Just as you did this morning in your own time of meditation. To ask such questions of oneself you must be prepared to be brutally honest with yourself.

Do not allow your own ego to judge my son. Always, allow the heart to take precedence. Follow your heart always. That is the way to the truth. For it is your inner knowing speaking directly to you."

S.H. "It is sad that so many people struggle with an idea of or have a lack of belief in their own self-worth. One of the things which I have learnt in my own life, is the importance of our own self-belief.

This especially, if we want to achieve something great. Something of stature. Something which stands out from the rest."

H.S. "Yes, my son. Greatness does take self-belief. But, also doing something for the right reason in order for greatness to be achieved. When something is done out of love it is magnified tenfold. It will always come back to you. What you give you receive. This is divine law and karma."

S.H. "How should we define 'KARMA'?"

H.S. "To reap what you sow is a good analogy. What you do to others will come back to you. Use the mantra.
    'I will treat others as I wish to be treated'. Then you will not go wrong. It is quite simple my son."

S.H. "I do wish more people lived this way i.e. with this idea in mind. If everyone did the world would instantly become a much safer and more peaceful place to live. Why isn't that yet the case after so many thousands of years humanity has been around?"

H.S. "Greed and avarice my son. Selfishness, a lack of thought for others. Fundamentally, a lack of spiritual awareness and ultimately a lack of compassion and love for others. False belief and erroneous judgement. A belief that some are better, more special or more deserving than others. A belief by many that they are the body. That they only live once. These are the mistakes so many make in their thinking and their behaviour. This book is one of the many sources of the type of wisdom some people still need to learn. To digest. To act upon."

S.H. "Thank you. Of course, they do not need to read this or anything else, I believe.
    Inside each of us we can access such knowing and wisdom.

Through our conscience and intuition, our inner teacher. We must but listen and follow it always.

It is such a shame, a tragedy that we are not taught this in schools, in my opinion. We are taught to follow our own minds, our own thoughts. By that we are taught our minds are the route to our wisdom. Not something deeper such as our inner feelings or our heartfelt ability to know. I suppose in essence because these are touching on religious teachings. We live, certainly in the west, in a secular state of being almost. We are sub-consciously taught to ignore such whimsical follies, as a 'feeling', 'don't trust that, it is nothing, it is nonsensical rubbish'."

H.S. "Yes my son that is so. Yet these feelings do not go away. They do not go away because they are integral to the essence of your eternal nature. Who you truly are. The feelings come from the divine connection within you. It is this higher thought, that operates at the speed of light not 'egoic' thought from the mind.

It operates at a different frequency to thoughts from the mind. All possess this ability. It is inherent within you all. Many shut it out. They do not trust. Instead doubt its ability to be accurate.

Women often use their intuition more than men. This is generally, because they are more inclined to keep an open heart and show more compassion towards others, than many men. They are more open and receptive to their own feelings and more inclined to follow and trust their own inner promptings.

Women would make much better rulers of your governments than men for these reasons. If only men had more trust in them to allow this shift. But you know, the energy shift that has been going on for many years now is one of a feminine vibrational energy to facilitate changes. It is one of the reasons for the emancipation of so many women around your world. Where it is least in evidence you will also find that there is still the most unrest and cruelty evident. When you see a shift in how women are treated in these areas, you will know true changes are happening globally, my son."

S.H. "Can we talk a bit about religion now. I have studied a few religions, but not to a great depth. However, from my own limited knowledge of the teachings concerning the different religions which exist around the world, what I notice is that there seems to be a golden thread, so to speak, which runs through them all. The thread is an analogy of the similarities between them.

I personally do not follow any one religion. The nearest belief I have is that 'golden thread' which I see as running through them all."

H.S. "Yes, my son, that is a good and accurate analogy. There is much truth in the religions of your planet. Some however, have been changed over the years to suit certain individuals according to their own beliefs and for their own reasons. Some have become confusing, illogical and convoluted. Religion is not a good thing or a bad thing. It has helped many and it has also led to suffering by many, where dogma has attached it to certain systems of belief within the confines of some religions.

Talking about different religions is like walking on egg shells my son and I suggest it is not the best subject to go into here, in this particular format of writing. Its essence is wrapped up in the dogma and ideology of history and historical figures from your past."

S.H. "I would like to speak however if it is okay, about Jesus. I feel a great affinity with Jesus. If I could choose to go back in time and meet just one person, it would without doubt, be Jesus. I feel a great deal of love for him for some reason. I don't know why exactly. I feel as if somehow, I knew him a bit. I hope that does not make me sound like a crazy person?"

H.S. "My son, no not at all. In truth, you have known him as did many in that lifetime. You were around in the Middle East at that time my son. You also were from a poor family and lived in a village not too far from Nazareth, where Jesus grew up. You met him on a few occasions when you were both very young and you knew that he was a <u>very</u> special person."

S.H. "Because I believe totally in the concept of reincarnation, I can believe that is true. I have for much of my life felt a strong affinity to Jesus even though I grew up in a non-religious family."

H.S. "My son the loving brother known to you as 'Jesus' was indeed a great spiritual being who brought much love into your world, as you know. The essence of that being still does great things on higher vibrational being where the energy that manifested in human form known as 'Jesus' now resides. It is possible to connect to this vibration for some if you ask at times such as during your meditation, as indeed you have in the past."

S.H. "Yes, I remember that on one occasion. It was a very beautiful experience for me.

Can I also ask about the Avatar Sri Sathya Sai Baba, whom I visited twice in India, before he died?

I feel I derived much benefit from my visits to see him. I feel that he was a being like Jesus. If not more powerful even. I know of the controversy about him, towards the end of his life. However, I spent quite a lot of time with others in his presence. I know without doubt that he was not an ordinary human being. I could always see a halo around his head. Can you comment on Sai Baba please?"

H.S. "Yes, my son. Sai Baba was a cosmic avatar. A full incarnation of the Godhead. He had full knowledge of his true essence. There was no limitation to his powers my son. You were blessed to be in his company on those occasions. Your wishes will be completed as they were affirmed. It is difficult to put into words the rarity of your good fortune just to have been in his aura my son. From this experience, there will be benefits to your soul's progress for lifetimes to come. This is as much as we can say on this matter at this time, here my son."

S.H. "Thank you. I have just remembered a saying which I read somewhere. 'Before enlightenment chop wood and collect water. After enlightenment chop wood and collect water.'

I understand this saying, though I would not like to say that I am an enlightened being. However, I do believe that I am an eternal spiritual being, as are all of us. My own life has proved that to me from one experience I once had. The saying about the water and the wood, I can relate to, because after you feel that you have assimilated certain life changing truths, life just goes on as normal. With its usual problems and fears. At least it does for me.

I feel I had to go on a massive inner journey to find my true self, only to be back in the regular world. The main benefit for me is, I feel and know that I am a part of creation and not just a separate individual encased in a physical body. That is nice to know. But, you even get used to that realisation after a while. Part of me wants to keep on growing spiritually as a person."

H.S. "My son you have indeed come far in your own soul's growth in this lifetime to date. You have had your own challenges and difficulties. You have come through them, stronger and wiser for the experience. It is only now you feel that you are putting much of what you have learnt into practice and for the benefit of others.

However, we would say to you that you have been doing this for many years i.e. helping and serving others wherever you could. Sometimes at great risk to yourself during your many years in your previous profession as a uniformed police officer. During those years, you helped many in ways that you will never know or understand.

My son, this book will further that good work in helping to lead some other people through and out of their suffering and those around them. In helping to change the attitude of a few, you will help many more through the simple words in this book my son."

S.H. "Thank you. My main reason for wanting this book to be a success, is because I want to help to make this world a better place in which to live."

H.S. "We know that this is your heartfelt desire. That is why we are helping you to write it my son. Just as many others are helped by the divine spirit, to spread love, compassion and forgiveness to others."

S.H. "I seem often, to still have some difficulty during this process with thinking of pertinent and interesting questions, to ask within this dialogue. Particularly at the start of each daily writing session. That is unless I have a pre-arranged question. I try obviously to think of questions which the readers themselves would want to ask, if in my position. At the time of asking, I must try to suspend my own opinions and beliefs. This can be difficult at times to do. Could you give some guidance please?"

H.S. "My son. Firstly, welcome back to this writing process. It is more about your own connection each time. When you struggle for a question to ask here, you are using the left side of your brain. Your logical mind. The answers are from the right side, the intuitive or perhaps, we should say the 'gateway' to the answers you receive. What we would suggest, is to try to see no division between questions and answers. Use the same process for the questions as you do the answers. Allow the questions, where practicable to be given to you as well."

S.H. "Thank you. I will try that. Why do so many people find it difficult to use and trust their intuition over the logical mind?"

H.S. "Because, that is their upbringing or what they have been taught most to trust. You my son, over the years have taught yourself as much as possible to be in tune with your other senses. To listen and trust them for advice and guidance. Yes, your meditations have helped to teach trust in this inner process. Many, in fact most people, do not do this my son."

S.H. "Yes, I know. I am conducting this writing process each day in a hotel which I like to visit. It is difficult at times such as when it is busy. Due to interruption. But for various reasons it suits me."

H.S. "It is good practice to attempt this process in a busy environment. We know it can also be difficult. Your mind can switch off from distraction, if you allow it to."

S.H. "Yes, as I have discovered."

H.S. "What do you hope to achieve most from this book being published my son?"

S.H. "Firstly, just to complete it and to see it in book form will be a success for me. To see it published by a reputable company will be a success. To know it will be read by many people, an even greater success. However, the greatest success for me would be to know, however perhaps I never will know, that a certain number of people will wake up to a deeper spiritual essence within themselves.

I am trying to let go of my desire or hope for any change in such people. I am trying to trust that if they wake up to their true nature, then change will inevitably follow."

H.S. "Yes, that is good. Allow the process to unfold in eternal trust. God will guide those who are ready for such a book containing this information. Divine synchronicity occurs always my son. This includes all the processes in the manifestation of producing a book."

S.H. "What I missed about this process, yesterday for example, was that when I was sitting in this room, I tried to write but could not do so, as there were two ladies talking next to me. Their conversation was about matters which I always find disturbing to listen to. They were talking about the cancer one of their husbands had suffered with for years. I am a bit of a worrier, especially with topics such as illness. I felt almost as if these women wanted me to clear off and go, paranoid as it sounds, as I was sitting next to them both."

H.S. "My son indeed nothing happens by coincidence. You took the topic of conversation as a reason to leave early. You did not want to hear their conversation. There was an element on their part of revelling in a drama which was not their own drama. Both women tend to compete, who has the biggest drama to share with the other. Neither are aware of such. This is because both are competitive characters and wanted to hold the attention of the other. This as you know, is a very common human trait. Each person places more value on their drama than another's drama. Even if they are discussing a drama which may have been upsetting. Their intention is to hold on to the other person's energy. By feeding off the other's energy it reinforces their own sense of self. Their own self-importance. People need to feel a sense of self-importance. They need this to feel external validation. If they do not receive this they feel a lack. A lack of being needed. A lack of being loved. So, they take energy from others. This is at a subconscious level, to feel needed and this feeds into their own self-worth. Most people if they do not feel needed by others have little self-worth. Not all people of course. The aim of self-realisation is just that. The realisation that the self is enough. The self alone provides all the love and joy and fulfilment without 'another'. This does not mean that everyone should live like a 'loner'. It means that you do not need to seek self-validation from without but to discover it within your own selves. You are enough. You are complete alone. The paradox is, you never are, truly alone. It is not possible. God is always present within if you allow yourself to feel its presence, my son."

S.H. "Thank you. This was a timely reminder for me about yesterday's session where I was unable to write. Also, I missed not connecting with the peaceful energy which accompanies the process of writing these words. When they are being given to me it is like when I have received a healing from a good healer. It is like, receiving or eating healthy food. It is a joy being part of this writing process for this reason, as well as getting these words on paper. I feel uplifted after each session. So, I suppose when it doesn't happen, I miss it!"

H.S. "Yes my son, but know that the energy is there waiting and is at your disposal always. However, these words do come through on a particular vibration. This is a vibration of love, of a high order. This is only possible because you are humble enough to receive such. You have prayed many times to be used in this way for the spiritual upliftment of others. So, it is not surprising one of the effects is self-upliftment also."

S.H. "Yes, indeed. Can we now speak about our fears or phobias with which many suffer?

What is the best way to face our own many varied fears or phobias, which can cause blockages, keeping us from joy and fulfilment in our own lives?"

H.S. "My son, each of you will face many challenges and obstacles in your own lives as you know too well. Courage is the key. You need to find courage within yourselves to face your own inner demons, whatever they may be. To find love and inner peace, requires non-judgement of self and others. It requires unconditional love for self and others. Letting go of old pains and patterns, through letting go in turn, of old habits of thought and action, which are not beneficial to self or other beings.

To reach the goal of love and peace, the moment must be accessible, through awareness of the present moment. Staying in the present moment as much as possible. By learning mindfulness through meditation is most helpful."

S.H. "There is a lot there. Each of these topics could be a book or at least a chapter. How to access them and to learn them, could take lifetimes literally, for some people. Unconditional love for example. It sounds so easy and yet, I am sure most find that a big one. I do try my best to be unconditionally loving but find it challenging at times."

H.S. "Yes, we understand that and the reasons why. But it is necessary for peace in your world. To love others wherever possible despite their behaviour. The other is a part of you at the deepest level. To harm another mentally, physically or emotionally means you are harming yourself also. Consciousness is one. All of consciousness is connected, there is no separation. Only mental separation through a suspension of belief. This does not affect truth."

S.H. "If you find it hard to let go of old hurts and pain which prevent you loving another deeply, in say an intimate relationship. What is the easiest way to let go of that blockage?"

H.S. "My son the easiest way is through forgiveness towards those who you believe caused that hurt and pain. Until forgiveness is given the blockage will remain my son."

S.H. "So the one hurting will have to have reached the point to want to forgive otherwise they won't, will they?"

H.S. "Correct. Sometimes this needs pointing out to the person concerned who needs to forgive and let go. The forgiveness opens the heart to allow love to flow through the heart chakra."

S.H. "How come someone with such a problem can love their child but not a member of the opposite sex when they are in a relationship with them?"

H.S. "This can be for several reasons of course. It can also be because the person is afraid of emotional intimacy of a sexual nature on a psychological level. This also can be for a variety of reasons. If vulnerability is the reason then the person needs to make small individual steps by facing and experiencing that which makes them feel vulnerable until the feeling no longer returns and move through the process gradually, sitting with the emotion when it surfaces until it subsides and honouring it. It is human nature to try to avoid things which make you feel uncomfortable. Yet to overcome certain feelings if they are causing problems such as within a relationship, then they can only be healed through facing them and working through them."

S.H. "You mention meditation about helping with mindfulness. What other methods can you suggest helping us stay in the moment?"

H.S. "If you want to remain in the present moment you must be 'present'. To be present means to be aware of your own thoughts and emotions as well as what is occurring around you simultaneously. To do this is an art and takes practice. It is something to keep moving towards. The more you practice it the better you become at being 'present' in the moment.

A good way is to do the things you enjoy most. When you do, you will find that they 'lock' you into the present moment with least effort. Try to be aware of your thoughts and feelings, or lack of them at such times. To do so will teach you how it feels to be fully present. When you know the feeling of being fully present you will know what the feeling is that you are trying to obtain at other less enjoyable times i.e. such as waiting at the doctors or dentist!"

S.H. "I would like to talk more about being present, in the present moment.

Also, I would like to talk a bit about the essence of what 'time' actually is and how real it is!"

H.S. "In truth only the present moment actually exists. The past and the future are concepts. They are not real in the truest sense. You live in one long continuous present moment. You do not believe this to be true. Humanity in general does not believe this to be true. This is because you experienced yesterday and you will most likely experience tomorrow. What I can tell you is that after your physical body ceases to exist your spirit or soul will experience non-time. It will be aware that time exists in the physical world. But not the spiritual dimension. When you are totally in the moment it can feel as if time itself is suspended and for the same reason. It is like time stops. It is when you are so locked into the moment perhaps because you are so enjoying it or so engrossed in whatever the experience is. I am sure many of the readers of this book will be able to relate to this experience.

In what you would call heaven, there is no sense of time. This is also due to the fact that your being and your senses are different. You do not then have a physical body only an etheric body. This is ageless, timeless, eternal, the consciousness which is what you are, which in truth is 'God' or whatever label you wish to use for 'God' is eternal as you no doubt have heard many times before."

S.H. "I can sort of understand the concept of what you are saying. I often feel now that instead of moving through time myself, that instead, time is moving through me. A bit like, if you were still always and never moved your body at all. This feeling of time moving through you would be even more exaggerated. Is this because as I get older I am more aware of my spirit than before?"

H.S. "Yes, in part this is true my son. You are learning to be more present than you once were. So, you sense things differently to how you once did. You are right, because your true essence is eternal i.e. your soul, your spirit. That part of you is ageless. Something ageless which is not connected to time, lives outside of time. It is not touched by time in the way the physical body is. Your soul has been encased in a multitude of physical bodies. It remains pure and untarnished at the deepest level. You are sensing time moving through your spirit.

If you stood next to a railway track in a desert where there was no movement except the occasional train rushing past you and there was continuous daylight your concept of time would be measured by the passing trains. You would have little else to measure time against. This sense of time moving through you would be more palpable but because of all the movements in life such as day and night, the sense that it is you who moves through time and not the other way around is reinforced.

What we know you are aware of even more clearly, is that on some level you do know that you exist in one continuous present moment i.e. you are always living in the present moment even though you and most people are not actually 'present' mentally in the present moment."

S.H. "So at some level everything that has happened or will happen is happening now."

H.S. "Yes. Not only that, every possibility of what could be happening is happening now. You live in a multiverse of possibilities all simultaneously occurring right now. Your brain only experiences one for health reasons.

You have many different possible futures. It depends which one you choose in each moment."

S.H. "I find this concept very difficult to understand and believe. Just to think about it sends my brain a bit crazy."

H.S. "That is why you have no concept of it. It is why the brain shuts it out. In the very same way and for the same reason most people have no concept of their own past lives. To protect yours and their own mental health. You are unusual my son in being able to open your mind sufficiently for this process to occur. Some will think you are crazy just writing this book in this way. However, you are able to make the adjustment in your mind /brain to allow this information to reach these pages through your written word. It is just a very subtle adjustment in your consciousness of stepping aside and trusting in the process. Is it not my son?"

S.H. "Yes, it is, that is right. When I am writing this, it flows so easily, I can only just, keep up with the flow of the information. I am totally in the moment. It feels as if someone has stopped the 'clock of time'. I feel enthused and regenerated. I feel after I have completed the writing, not drained but instead, as if I had sat in the presence of a healer and received a spiritual healing at the same time, during the writing process. The words are just channeled through me. I think a lot of creative material is channeled. Whether it is writing, art or music. I love writing this. It is thinking of good, relevant or interesting questions which I find hardest to come up with. The answers just flow. They flash through me!"

H.S. "Indeed my son, you are a good channel for this type of work. We thank you for taking the time out of your day, to bring through information to help many others who over time will read these words and will find them most helpful in their own awakening and remembering who they truly are, also my son."

S.H. "Thank you for the kind supportive words.
However, why should we as individuals, aspire or try to be

'present'. Why should we aim to be in the present moment as opposed to thinking, planning, imagining, being creative with our minds and have positive thoughts rather than worrying obviously?

I am playing devil's advocate here of course!"

H.S. "My son, the main benefit is the fact that you are connected to the source, as you are now. You are in the moment, writing down these words. The purpose being to spread the information contained here to help and uplift others who are drawn to these words.

It is the choice of the individual as to whether to be present or not. Indeed, how present they wish to aspire to be. It is an art obtained through practice. A skill if you like. It requires a discipline of thought. It is made easier when the body and mind are healthy and in harmony. It is a reflection of the consciousness of the individual concerned, as to how present you are, the majority of the time. This is not a reflection of how 'good' or 'bad' the individual's character is. Nor is it necessarily a reflection of the wisdom held by the individual concerned. However, awareness is a reflection of the openness of the mind of the individual. Without an open mind, you cannot grow in awareness. So be open always my son, to new knowledge, new wisdom. Be flexible, like grass in the wind blowing each way without resistance.

Always, be led by your own intuition, your own inner teacher. If it resonates with your own inner truth, your own inner knowingness, follow that. If it does not then move on. It is not for you. Trust yourself. The true 'self'. The true self is never less than a heartbeat away. It dances with you. It shares your breath as much as it shares the wind and sunshine upon the lands and shores of your Earth and all Earth's.

You live on a planet of choice. So, choose wisely and continue to guide others to also choose from love and compassion. The choice then will always come from wisdom. That is because it is a choice made from love. This is the same as the source. The source is love and that at the deepest level is what you are. It is what sustains all of creation."

S.H. "Are most of the problems in the world caused by people not following their heart's, when making decisions about things?

Is it because the world is still full of a lot of selfish rather than selfless people?"

H.S. "My son, each person is at their own stage of growth in consciousness. Some are further down the road towards their own self-realisation, some less so. Each in their own time. Society obviously has a bearing on the consciousness of the group. However, as much as society is a reflection of the people who make up that society, so, in turn the majority of the group are drawn to others of a similar level of consciousness. It is the law that others are drawn to those who they most resonate with themselves."

S.H. "Yes, I can see that. Is the consciousness of the planet and of humanity being raised now by external sources such as by the planet itself and the Sun?

I ask this, as I have learnt to believe in the 'Gaia' theory, that the earth itself is a living entity. Along such lines, I believe the Sun itself, also has its own consciousness too."

H.S. "The consciousness of humanity is affected by your Earth and your Sun. Yes, on a vibrational level. However, it is more by the Sun than the Earth. The Earths vibration is being raised by the Sun. This Earth in turn, as its vibration raises, has the effect of raising the vibration of <u>ALL</u> that lives on your Earth. The raising of temperatures, is in part caused by the Sun. Mainly so in fact. To a lesser effect but also as a result of the burning of fossil fuels to the degree they are used, there is also a slight warming effect. The effect of fossil fuels is more harmful as regards the pollution it causes to the land, yourselves and the atmosphere however.

The Sun's light is also a vibration of love. The love raises consciousness. The light raises the temperature. The Sun has existed for a long time. Yet the Sun is also eternal. This does not mean it will shine for ever. But its consciousness will forever shine, as that is eternal. Remember, 'time waits for no man', is the saying. This is true. Yet your essence remains the same. Eternal. You are eternal. Your essence is eternal. Your body is finite. Your body is not eternal. It will decay. It will cease to be. Your essence will never cease to be. Neither of course will the essence of all those reading these words. Your body moves with time. Your essence, your spirit, your soul, your consciousness, the divine you, they are all names, these things remain. Focus on the 'inner view' not the outer view. The inner journey, the inner work is the key. If you do not try to heal yourself, how can you heal others?

Love is the key to this work. Love holds all the answers. When you are 'present' in the present you are in the presence of that, of which is who you all truly are. Express this love each and every day, not just towards others but to yourself also. Be kind and loving to yourselves also. If you are unkind to your own selves, your own body, how can you help others. To embody change is to embody love."

S.H. "People I see, are so caught up in their daily work so much of the time. Chasing a living. Chasing money to live or even just survive to realise a lot of these truths. That is, if they are even interested in these spiritual topics. I don't blame them. I understand this. We in the west live in such a secular society. I feel there is such a spiritual famine in the western world. Yet, I sense a big increase in the levels now of the awareness and compassion in the younger generation to my own. I hope and pray that they are also helping to usher in a new age of fairness, love and respect for our Earth and all that reside on her."

H.S. "Yes, my son this is a time of great change indeed. The change has been occurring for some time. There is a 'feminine' energy flooding your planet influencing all of creation, which is helping with this process. This will help to ensure peace in your world which is the most important factor for the survival of your planet. Without peace, any growth in individuals will be futile. Peace is the sustenance of the soul. Divinity will ensure the outcome of peace on your planet my son, have no fear."

S.H. "You said there, that peace will be the outcome. Does that not over-rule something you said previously, that this is a 'planet of choice'?

That we have free will. Does that not include allowing humanity to destroy itself?"

H.S. "My son, humanity does have free will to do as they please. However, that does not include the capacity to also eliminate peace on your planet. If humanity disappeared peace would not. Of course, your world then be more peaceful and all souls would exist elsewhere. They would still exist."

S.H. "But will humanity eventually destroy itself?
Would God allow that to happen?"

H.S. "It could happen if humanity allowed it to happen. However, it is most unlikely as the rate of consciousness increasing, which will continue, should ensure a greater peace prevails than you have now. This is a time of changing the guard. The batten is being passed from one epoch to another. The digital age, the computer age is the signifier of this. The connection it allows humanity, will allow greater peace rather than greater conflict. There is far more goodness in your world than bad. This is the main reason that peace will be the outcome. The armies for peace, far outnumber those who would prefer conflict between different races, or countries or even religions."

S.H. "What can the individual do to play their part in helping to make the world a more peaceful place?"

H.S. "By embodying peace themselves. In their actions, thoughts and words. Serving and helping others wherever they can. Especially when opportunities to do so arise. Even the smallest service to others has a ripple effect which spreads in ways unknown to you my son."

S.H. "For someone suffering from say, stress and anxiety on a regular basis. What would you suggest?"

H.S. "This is a very open ended question. There are so many possible factors dependant on the individual in question. The answer can be different for many. However, in general this answer would be true for all.

Focus on 'peace' at all times. When you are at peace stress and anxiety will melt away. If you are at peace you cannot be either stressed or anxious. Find what brings you peace and enjoy that wherever possible. Those things which have the opposite effect, as much as possible, eliminate them from your life."

S.H. "You have mentioned the importance of being in the present moment. How can we remember and be mindful to keep bringing our attention back to the present moment?"

H.S. "Peace comes from within you. Within you lies the connection. Not outside of you. Though in reality there is no outside of you because there is no separation at the deepest level.

This quest for peace is the challenge you all face in your world. Keep your attention on what brings you peace and what does not. Where possible always choose peace. Sometimes this is not possible such as during an emergency or conflict. But even during the most challenging of events, peace is achievable, though it may be difficult. Remember you are not your mind. You are not your body. You are not your fears. You are living conscious awareness. You can focus on peace or conflict and anxiety. You choose where the focus of your attention lies. This is the first part of the conscious journey towards peace. Each time you notice your mind or body sensations moving away from peace, steer it back to peace. In your mind, to assist this process say, 'I choose peace'. This in itself, is a reminder for you personally, that you can choose what thoughts and feelings you focus your mind upon. The mind is the bridge. The builder between your two worlds. The etheric world and the physical world. Your thoughts and actions create your reality. If you want to bring an idea you have into reality, you must keep your focus and intent using your words, thoughts and actions, as if they were the building materials to create your own desires. For example, you are creating this book. For a long time, you have wanted to write a book. You have held the thought and therefore the intent to bring it to fruition. You have moved from the thought and intent to write a book, into action and you have started to write it. You have started to create the book. Through your perseverance which you are using, the book is being made manifest. Keep using your own imagination, using the power of visualization and see the finished book. See it printed in hardback, published for sale. See it as a success, purchased by many and helping them to bring greater insight and peace into their own lives.

You can use this process to create and bring whatever you want, into your life. Believe implicitly in the process. The greater the belief, the greater the power you will have and see what comes into your life.

Use these skills for good and to enhance the lives of the many. Use this power, which you all possess to make life better for all. This is your birth right. Take back you power. Do not let your doubt, steal your power, as a thief in the night would do so. Shine my son. Shine your light into the world. All can shine equally, choose to shine. Radiate your peace. Radiate your joy to uplift and raise the consciousness of others. Realise self. Realise truth. Truth will set you all free from your fear and doubts. These are merely different shadows on the veils of your own illusions, shared by many."

S.H. "Thank you. There was a lot there. It is about learning to live in a different way really. It feels like walking through life awake and not asleep. I feel that, for so much of my life I have in a way been sleep walking through my life. Now I feel much more alert and awake, as I do so. It has been so difficult to reach the point of awareness which I have now reached. It has been my choice for many years, to try to wake up as much as possible, to a higher level of consciousness, if you like. Yet, it has been an incredible challenge, to reach where I am now in myself. I know there is further to go. The mind and the emotions of fear, anxiety and doubt and a lack of self-belief have held me back.

Also, life's challenges such as broken or difficult relationships have also been a great distraction from my own progress despite the things they can also teach us.

I mention this only in empathy with others who read these words and may feel this way. Most people will face the same challenges as they are part and parcel of the life experience. Many people do not aspire to 'wake up' or would not understand the principle, thinking that if they are not physically asleep, then by definition they must already be 'awake'. Yet, I suppose such people would obviously not be drawn to a book such as this one at this time?"

H.S. "Yes my son 'at this time', being the operative words here. All people change and grow, yet at their own pace. Where you are down the road in terms of spiritual growth towards enlightenment is secondary. The most important factor is to try to move forwards in these terms. It is really a remembering process. You are remembering your true self. When you remember this truly, you will feel you were only 'asleep' for the shortest time. Once you remember you will not forget again."

S.H. "I notice that when I feel fear, or anxiety, or doubt, it is I find, more difficult to be fully present. My mind gets caught up in my own drama's. Whether, they be about health concerns, money worries or whatever. This I find so frustrating because I have spent so much of my adult life in this way. How can I be more present at challenging times such as this?

How can others do likewise i.e. find peace when bogged down in day to day worries?"

H.S. "My son, this is a common question many would ask, aside from the spiritual side of life's discovery. It is the mastering of all the skills we have been speaking about so far. We know it is not easy when the mind is distracted in this way.

Distract the mind in any other way. Like you are doing now as a positive distraction. Consciously choose peace over fear or worry. Say to yourself in your own mind, 'I choose peace', until peace returns to your own mind my son."

S.H. "We have spoken about connecting or reconnecting with spirit within. Waking up to who we truly are which is consciousness. A consciousness we all share at the deepest level. This should help us all feel more connected and peaceful.

I would like to ask more questions about feeling more connected to the environment and the Earth as this is our home. It is no good being in balance with all of our being, if we are not living in balance with the Earth. Can you say more about this relationship please?"

H.S. "Good question my son. A most pertinent one too. At this time, there is a lot of discussion in your news about the poor air quality in many of your cities around your planet. How this affects the health of human beings. It does indeed have an impact on the health and well-being of those being exposed regularly to toxins in your air. This is from pollution related to traffic and industrial waste and power production using fossil fuels. Your planet needs to keep the focus on clean energy, renewable energy such as wind and solar to replace the other methods which cause harmful pollution to your atmosphere and your environment. The younger generations to your own in many ways are more concerned and aware than your own. The effects of pollution affect not just humans of course but the rest of the animal kingdom as well.

At this time, human beings are the guardians of your planet and it is down to you to take care of it. As human consciousness has grown in the last few decades great changes have and are continuing to take place. These will continue my son, have no fear. The two go inevitably hand in hand. One is leading to the other. As the consciousness shifts so does the effect on your environment on many levels.

Each individual has their own role to play in your world. As each follows their own inner promptings they will be drawn to the purpose which has attracted them to your world at this time. Those whose calling is this field of scope will be drawn unto it. Your own is different. At this time, it is compiling these words to help uplift and to inspire others on their own spiritual journey. For some it will be purely about cleaning up the environment in various ways. Each has their own gift to use and express in different ways so a person does not need to feel guilty if such a role, is not theirs. You all can help in your own small ways. Such as thinking about the type of fuel you use to travel. How you heat your homes and dispose of your own rubbish.

The production of plastic should be reduced and replaced wherever possible, also recycled. If you continue to pollute your waters and your oceans the effects on the marine life will continue to harm not just them but also your own selves through the food chain. Through this chain humanity are linked, as if by karma, as they are affected by such things as toxins and plastic particles being ingested in the same way as fish are to not just their detriment but humanity's also."

S.H. "I would like to return to the topic of the Higher-Self which we spoke of earlier in the book. Last night I read something similar to the topics discussed in this dialogue. I found it very interesting.

I could tell the message and the energy of those words were similar to the message here.

I trust and believe in these words and in the process through which they are delivered. I believe in the purpose of their message which is to help awaken others to who they truly are. That they are spirit in a material world."

H.S. "Indeed you are all an ocean of spirit in a material world. You are an ocean of consciousness lapping at the shore.

You, straddle two worlds my son. Most, still by far have yet to step and have both feet in the water. They are unaware the world they experience is in truth the illusion. They think the world is real. Yet the world is the dream. The world of the ethereal is the true world for this is the eternal spring from which the spirit springs. It is the world of spirit from which your essence sprung and to which it returns once your bodies cease to function. The life force which animates all being and all beings is shared by all. You are all here to experience creation through the mind of God. Your experiences are also Gods experience. You have free will. Free choice to choose what they should be. If you choose love each step of the way, heaven will be here on earth for you now. If you wish to experience hell here on earth, then yes, you may experience that also if you so choose.

My son, many in certain parts of your real physical world are experiencing that now. Whether through war, famine or both. Many are also experiencing heaven.

There are many reasons why each person is at any time experiencing what they are experiencing. At the deepest level, they have chosen this. With many, their souls chose to incarnate in those places where conflict has arisen. Their souls knew in advance of the difficulties which laid ahead. For karmic reasons the choices are made. If a person doubts these words then they are free to do so. Yet choose they did.

However, to get to the point of the question. Yes, the energy of these words is the same. Your Higher-Self is the same. The

Higher-Self is an aspect of who you are. It is the diamond of your soul. If you like, the facets of this diamond are like the many lives each of you live. In this case lives connected to your soul. The diamond is part of an ocean without end which is the true essence of you, of what you all are and share.

The 'diamond' that you are has not incarnated. The facets of energy, consciousness have. The energy or consciousness which is the source of these words is an aspect of you as stated. Therefore, on a certain level you could argue that this dialogue, this conversation is you speaking to you. But a you from another aspect or frequency of being. When you listen to your inner promptings. Your intuition. Your sixth sense. Call it what you like, it is your soul. Your Higher-Self communicating with you has the highest frequency of thought capable unto you. It is information through inner knowing. It is information carried to you at the same subtle frequency of love. It is the reason you leave these sessions feeling lighter and uplifted. The words come to you on the frequency of the currents of love from the greater ocean of your being.

You have enabled yourself, your physical mind i.e. your beliefs and judgements to step to one side. This enables this information to pass through to you and be written down here as the words appear before you. Like a dictation. The fact the energy and frequency remain the same is proof that the source is real and true to yourself. The more you can allow the energy to flow through you the greater the ability for change. Change for the better for yourself and others. This energy can help to awaken others as the frequency touches their soul through these words.

If the words resonate with the reader, they will feel in their hearts, the same energy, you feel now. They will feel a sense of peace and calm envelope them as the information is processed by their own intellectual capacity. They will also assimilate alongside these words a feeling of knowing the truth of these words beyond their own understanding. It will be as if they are receiving information about something they always knew deep down. Yet at the surface level had forgotten. An experience similar to your own, back along on your own journey towards remembrance."

S.H. "Thank you. For some reason, I am assuming that most readers of this book will be young. In their twenties or early thirties perhaps. But of course, they could be any age. I started to wake up to these 'truths' as well in my late twenties."

H.S. "My son, all people are at a different stage on their own inner journey. People of all ages will be drawn to these words. Let go of the end result my son and allow what will be, to be. This project is like raising a child my son. Treat it as such. Bringing the book into fruition is the raising process. Once completed and released into the world, merely forget about it where possible and trust 'God' to allow it, to find its way into the hands of those who are seeking out the information it contains at that time. Your work will have been done as regards this project. If there is more to follow you will be prompted in that direction and if you choose in future days."

S.H. "I have wanted to write a book with a spiritual message for a long time even a novel, of course this one though not a novel, has a variety of different messages. My question today is, what does humanity need to address more than anything, now?"

H.S. "My son, good question. Humanity needs collectively to examine its conscience. As does the individual. This is on a moment to moment basis. If each person did this, your world would change from that moment.

You see, the reason for this would be that when you follow the 'still', small voice of the conscience, you are following the direction of the 'Highest-Self' within. The part of the inherent wisdom resident within all humans. My son, this voice will tell you all what is right and what is wrong. So many deny or ignore this voice within themselves to the detriment not only to themselves but others also of course.

However, if each of you open to this intuitive way of being led, follows the voice, each can bring about greater peace and harmony. Each will be a beacon of change towards greater peace and evolution of your world.

The younger generations to yourself, are naturally more open to this way of being. They will not need to be educated to follow their conscience as it will be more inherent within them, due to their own soul's evolution for most incarnating now are, what many would call 'old souls' here to help your planet at a time of great change.

Your own generation has been overall a quite selfish one. This is the reason so much violence and discord is still evident for all to see. However, the energy vibration on which these souls in the main incarnated with has ceased. Beings with a different soul vibration are attracted to the new vibration. This is higher, more feminine and gentle. Those who do not or cannot resonate with it are leaving their bodies in greater numbers than is usual. Their time here is done. They are making way for the younger more enlightened generations to bring in the changes they came here to make to your societies. The essence of these changes will be towards greater peace and equality around your world. There will of course be many pockets of resistance to this but the new will be the victors.

You will notice that the new generations of youth will be less drawn to the ways of vice or those lacking in virtue. They will be less focused on the material world and more drawn to the natural world. They will be more drawn to the countryside than cities. They will be less inclined to eat meat or drink alcohol or take drugs. For these reasons, they will be a generation of better health even than your own. They will be drawn to spirituality in the ways it unites rather than divides. They will be more accepting of different religions. They will help clean up your atmosphere's and environment. Plastic will be phased out of use. The worlds view will move toward global sharing rather than global taking and hoarding.

Seas will rise and borders will change and disappear and there will be much movement of populations around your globe. Instead of economic migrants you will have ecological migrants because of changes in topography and weather patterns. Some places will become too hot for many to stay. For the rest of your life these changes will be occurring my son. You will be witness to many. Pockets of resistance on many levels will be evident but doomed to failure. For this resistance is the energy of the past and will inevitably have to submit to the new as they are increasingly outnumbered. Those who have hoarded great amounts of wealth will lose it, if they do not give it to those in greater need. These changes will help with the consciousness of humanity rising and will also be largely because of this change in human consciousness. Humanity will evolve to a higher level of being."

S.H. "I am very pleased to hear these words and I pray that all this will come to pass. If my own small contribution through my efforts here and there help too, I will be very pleased to feel that maybe I have helped in this process of awakening those towards changes for the better for all.

However, I sometimes have the feeling that to date, that I have not achieved much in my life. Maybe, you could say under achieved, to date. I hear famous people on the radio or see them on the television. It is easy for any of us to compare ourselves and our achievements to others. Is this unwise?"

H.S. "My son. What would the purpose of comparison be. If not to feel better about one's own achievement. To do the opposite would be futile. Indeed, there are always greater and lesser persons. The measure of the comparison we would argue is not what one has achieved for oneself but for others. Indeed, even from the spiritual perspective of introspection and self-enlightenment the best use for any self-development in this field is regarding what greater help that you can give to enable others to either improve their lives or find a greater evolution in their soul's growth. Rather than measure your own achievements against others, measure your own development of self, where you once were on an inner level to where you either are now or wish to reach in your future. The most important journey towards achievement is the inner journey. The real achievement in this regard is in growth of spirit, wisdom and compassion. Then harnessing that growth to help and serve to do likewise."

S.H. "I suppose one of the issues is that there is a competitive spirit in most societies to do as well as you can materially for yourself and any family that you have as an adult. This is in part, to increase one's material prosperity and self-esteem or ego. This starts with parents towards their children and is so often learned behaviour it would seem. There is now an inter-generational competition as in my own country, the United Kingdom. The perception that many older people have more material gains, such as house ownership and pensions, than the younger generations. This just creates bitterness and resentment as it often does between individuals of similar generations. The financial and material interests, ethereal as they are due to their limited possession or ownership time wise is for this reason illusory. Yet that which is deeper such as our own growth is the real treasure. The real success especially, if used and shared. 'Be the change you want to see in the world', comes to mind. This I can see is of the greatest value. Prosperity can only be truly real if founded on peace and harmony."

H.S. "Yes, my son this is so. However, children are still taught in a similar fashion to that which they have been for the last few centuries. There are a few exceptions. Children are indoctrinated in your society to think like the society they are in. To behave like the society, they are in and to look towards financial success. Not their own spiritual success in terms of wisdom, growth and compassion for others. They are of course taught that they are separate except from their own family. Children are not truly taught but trained to think and behave like whatever the society is that they are in. Some break free from this indoctrinated thinking, some do not. However, your belief systems whatever they are, dependent on where you are raised, much more often act as mental prison bars, which limit your freedom and expression towards your true birth right, which is self-expression for what your heart and soul yearns. This is for love and peace primarily. However, if you are taught separation over global inclusion only conflict can result when global resources or the fear of shortages occur. This is the main reason for wars starting. A fear of lack or a greed of certain individuals for more, whether it be power or resources, often this is even about the power which the perception of having resources brings to the individuals, who perceive themselves to possess power over others is what corrupts and distorts the minds of those individuals most. For these things bring a greater and greater belief in their own greatness which increases their lust for greater power over others. Yet the power eventually always leads to self-destruction for the power is of the mind and not of the heart."

S.H. "How can society turn this around more successfully than we are doing at present. Is it about educating the young in a very different way, rather than training them to think and act like the generations which have gone before them?"

H.S. "Yes my son, otherwise you simply repeat the mistakes of old if they are trained to have the same mind-set. It stands to reason. They need to be taught differently in how to approach life and where their focus should be. Your young are not taught about the power of their own minds and how the mind creates their world. That mind is the builder. That they create their reality according to their own beliefs. They need to be taught how to use their beliefs to create the world they want to see. A shift in beliefs is the most important factor at any time. Then the action is reflected by the beliefs held and changes for the better will result. Obviously the greater the awareness of the individual the more likely they will be in tune with their wisdom.

This is love based not fear based. Therefore, decisions are birthed from love for their fellow man and good will be the result."

S.H. "How and why is mind the builder?
Is the mind the same as the personality?"

H.S. "No my son the personality is different to the mind. The personality is a group set of beliefs, attributes such as likes and dislikes and a mixture of the individual's experiences which form such.

The mind is, as the engine is to the car. The car is the personality, the engine drives it. In your case the mind is the power behind what your body does. The mind also has another attribute, few in your world understand or believe. The mind interacts with the consciousness around you including all other persons to assist bringing about that which the mind has been focused on with its own intent. The effect on others is at the subconscious level. It is the same as the law of attraction or repulsion. The mind can attract your desires to you or push them away. The mind has the power of manifestation of many things. The more focused the mind with the power of true belief, the more able or capable the individual who has reached this level of awareness becomes. When love is the driver of this intent, the mind is most powerful.

However, the power of the mind can be used for good or evil. What you reap you sow. That is the law of karma my son."

S.H. "So we can draw into our lives, things, people and experiences that we desire, simply with the power of our minds."

H.S. "Yes my son. For most this takes time to occur. For some more evolved souls it can be instant manifestation. That is very rare i.e. such as in the case of Jesus. However, due to the delay in that which is desired coming into your reality or experience 'you' are mostly unaware of how your own thoughts have helped to bring whatever it is into your life experience. In this case by 'you', we mean human beings generally. Again, it is about being 'aware' of your thoughts and intentions. How you focus them. To watch for the results of the manifestation of such. To allow and let go of such thoughts and intentions, to allow the universe to do its work for you. In the 'knowing comes the receiving' my son."

S.H. "So, let's use the creation of this book as an example. I have wanted to write or create it for many years. Only recently have I felt 'present' enough to do it. I will complete it. I trust it will reach those with whom it resonates most. At this time, I do not know who to approach with regards the publishing of this book. But I trust it will be so."

H.S. "My son, you have effectively answered your own question by the way you have phrased the question. As you well know, you have shown a positive trust in what you intend to manifest i.e. a book. You are revealing in the question also the important fact of non-attachment to the outcome by the process, in this case the publisher. That is who will fulfil this role ultimately to realise the book to the public at large. It is about not just, self-confidence in your own abilities but having confidence in the universe also doing its work for you."

S.H. "Since I was a teenager there has been within me a deep urge to discover through others and eventually by going within my own self, answers to the big questions in life.

Such as, who are we?

Why are we here, alive in human form?

What is the true purpose of our lives?

At the same time however, I am aware that many, possibly most people, do not seem that interested in these sorts of questions but the type of person drawn to a book such as this one, will be of course!

The point of the question though, is why are some people drawn to go on this inner journey and some are not? I cannot imagine myself, why some would have no interest to take this inner journey of self-discovery and all the rewards it can bring. This has been my own experience."

H.S. "My son all are different. All beings are on their own journey. None know of the other person's trials and tribulations they endure, often this includes direct family and even spouses. Each chooses the path they take and how they spend their own time. Yet life itself is a grand journey for all those who have the courage to undertake it. Many get lost along the way and so do not realise their full potential. Many souls do not even awaken sufficiently to remember they came into life for a reason or purpose. Instead, they get lost in the sensual and material pleasures which life can bring, be it fleeting ones.

My son, your own soul chose to awaken at a young age despite all the obstacles which were placed in your own way. Many were of your own making some were not. Your yearning has been for remembering the wisdom you have previously held in other incarnations. Your soul has an inner knowing of such and that has been the driving force to expand your consciousness to its full potential and to share this knowledge and wisdom with those who are drawn to the information.

Many of the other's you mention never achieved this level of awakening in other lifetimes and so the call is not as you feel it within yourself. This is the reason many are not drawn to a lifestyle such as yours my son. However, many souls are here for the same reason including those who have never previously attained high levels of conscious awareness. This is a time of a great shift in the consciousness of souls incarnated. They have chosen to be here primarily for this reason now. This is the main reason that the population is greater than at any other time my son."

S.H. "I have noticed also, that simply things, such as a sunny day can help us be more aware. Is this because at such times we are more open and loving?"

H.S. "Yes, my son. You feel more joy. When you are joyful and feeling love in your heart you will feel more loving towards others and connected to your physical world."

S.H. "I find it sometimes more difficult on overcast days
    To stay open and filled with joy. This cannot be uncommon?
Do some people choose to incarnate at a soul level in northern countries where there is less sunshine and day light for some sort of spiritual reason. I wondered about this today. In countries with a warmer climate, people who visit there from the United Kingdom often mention that the people in those countries often appear more warm and friendly in their disposition. This, even though they are most often poorer materially. To me it seems more testing for the soul as well as the body to be born into a country with a colder and harsher climate."

H.S. "Yes my son this is true. All souls have their own reason dependent on a variety of factors, for the choice of where their souls choose to incarnate. However, if you live in a harsher climate compared to others such as your own you must remember that each country has its own vibration and it is the vibration of the country, at the time you choose to incarnate that draws your soul to it the most. There is a collective consciousness in each country. Just as there is a collective consciousness in a family. You will be drawn to that. You will be especially drawn to the vibration of the individual who will be the mother who gives birth to your physical form. This will be most often, for karmic reasons. Karmic reasons for your own soul's growth and for that of whoever your mother, parents and family are at the given time."

S.H. "However, I guess ultimately it is not what we know, that counts. But what we do with what we know. How we use our wisdom to improve life for not just ourselves but for the benefit of our world and all of life upon it."

H.S. "Ultimately, that is true. However, although it seems paradoxical, though the problems in your world seem fraught and serious. There is still much to be happy about. To be joyful and light-hearted should still be your aim to share such with others as well as yourself.

The secret is to be filled with joy even in times of adversity as difficult as it sounds. Adversity is a state of mind. It is possible to be filled with joy even in a prison. In fact, at such a time this is how one would achieve inner freedom. Peace can be experienced within, whatever ones' external conditions.

This is a very high level of personal evolvement and personal awareness. It is possible. It takes skill and a great deal of personal awareness. This is not necessarily the aim of life. But it can be if you choose it to be. Bringing peace to others will bring an abundance of joy as well. Strive for both where possible. Do not berate yourself or others if you fail. Your intentions are ultimately more important than your achievements. Show the path. Point to the direction of travel, enable others to choose and make their own journey."

S.H. "So all of this knowledge, wisdom, teaching, call it what you will that I am endeavouring to capture and get down on paper is not really that complicated. To summarise: -

1) To awaken individuals to their own higher consciousness.
2) To help people remember there is no separation as we are all connected spiritually.
3) To connect with the joy and love inherent within themselves.
4) To love all and serve all."

H.S. "Yes my son."

S.H. "Yesterday, I walked across the road from the location where I have been writing this book and saw a notice outside a book shop. This being the following quote of Sophocles:

"One word frees us from all the weight and pain of life: that word is love".

Underneath was a picture of a polar bear cuddling a young girl to express this point.

For me, this captured in just a sentence, what the message is, that I am trying to relay contained within the pages of this book and in addition to the deeper spiritual aspect to what the 'essence' of love is. The quote mentioned had a big effect on me at the time.

I also reflected further, on that, if you asked a scientist to prove the existence of love using their usual criteria of proof that they would fail to do so. Yet they would for obvious reason decline from going so far as to say, love therefore does not exist!

My point is that you could use the same argument about the existence of God. They would argue, if they were an atheist, that God does not exist. Yet, many scientists would not as readily accept the existence for God as they would for the existence of love. Yet to me they are both obvious and walk hand in hand. One is proof of the other.

This is not so much a question rather a statement of course. One that I just wanted to get off my chest. Relevant, I feel at this point in the dialogue."

H.S. "Yes my son. It was also an example of synchronicity working in tandem with your own efforts. The notice you saw also showed the importance of 'expressing' love, not just 'understanding' more about its nature and reason for existence. You are all made from love. Love walks hand in hand with every aspect of you all. Whether you express that love or the opposite to love is your own choice in each moment. Choose love always."

S.H. "I would challenge the statement a bit however. I agree with the enormous power that love has. But for love to free us from all the weight and pain of the world is a big call. Take grief for example. Say, you are a single parent with no immediate family and your only child dies. The grief would be enormous and take a long time to heal. It is difficult, but I know you can still feel love inside if you open your heart to it. Yet, when you are filled with this sort of grief it is all consuming. At such times, it is very difficult to focus on love all the time to try to keep the grief at bay."

H.S. "Indeed my son. No one is saying it is easy, even with the help of love to avoid pain and grief. But you can in each moment you focus on love. But pain such as grief must be allowed. You need to pass through it, to experience it, to release it my son. It is one of the challenges of life."

S.H. "At this moment as I write, there are currently about twenty million people at risk of starvation in about five mainly African countries. The main reason for this, rather than being drought in this case, is war. This is going to result in a lot of grief for many people soon. What saddens me is that our media, especially newspapers or news on the internet allow very minor stories in comparison to totally overshadow this crisis. To me this can only be explained by selfishness rather than apathy. Many people do not care enough to do anything including some political leaders of some countries including some of the major ones."

H.S. "Yes my son. But if enough citizens, in enough countries took to the streets long enough things would change. Therefore, there is a large amount of apathy amongst the global populations of the world, as well my son."

S.H. "Yes, I know. Many people would just say, 'I am too busy trying to make a living for my family to go out in protest about people starving because of wars in other countries'. Plus, to stop it from happening, other countries would have to get involved and risk the possibility of getting caught up in these wars. They are I think, right in trying to avoid getting involved in such wars. That is unless it involves such crimes as genocide."

H.S. "Yes, rightly so. These are complex issues which can only be addressed globally by large organizations, such as the United Nations and political leaders need to ensure this pressure is kept up to ensure the necessary changes to help these people."

S.H. "At the deepest level, do the souls of people in such dire circumstances know that these sorts of challenges will be faced in their lifetime?"

H.S. "Yes, my son. They have chosen to incarnate in these places at such times. Not to experience pain, but to experience growth as a result of their experiences. This is true for you all. You have all chosen to be on your Earth for the experiences it brings for good or bad. Nothing is wasted. There are reasons behind all experiences, some of which cannot always be understood. That is until the people are ready to understand. That is the point when things change. We are talking about humanity itself reaching a certain level of group consciousness. Higher than it is at the current time in your experience."

five

The Ocean of Consciousness

S.H. "Are there other planets in the universe which are inhabited by life forms like human beings?"

H.S. "Yes, my son a great many."

S.H. "Is their consciousness more evolved than ours?"

H.S. "Some are, some are less so my son. You are all protected by distance and space. Other more technologically advanced civilizations are aware of your existence and have visited many times.

One of the laws of such highly evolved beings is to not interfere with your own evolvement. Each planet of course has its own history and story. In time your world will have direct contact with some of these beings. Some of these planets have been populated by beings far longer than your own. This is part of the reason for their greater evolvement and higher levels of awareness. It is because of these qualities that they have, succeeded and survived. These have chosen to live compassionately towards others as they have realised long ago that they are all part of the one consciousness which pervades and inhabits and indeed created all that is. They are also aware how dangerous to make contact with your world would be at this time. They leave well alone. Only to observe. There is no guarantee that they would interfere if your world was set on a course of self-destruction for this would be interference still in the group karma of your race. The human race."

S.H. "I know a whole book could be written on this topic of alien civilizations but though I have raised the question here myself. I do not feel it to be fruitful to go into more detail on the topic now. There is enough to be done in terms of evolvement of humanity here on Earth."

H.S. "Indeed my son."

S.H. "Has humanity reached a higher level of consciousness before the present time."

H.S. "No my son. Only as individuals and small groups in your history. The consciousness of the whole planetary population needs a critical mass globally to make that leap. This is what is occurring right now on your planet as we speak. However, it will last for a few decades yet. For most of the twenty-first century it will continue at great pace my son. This will not happen to everyone in a moment of time. To individuals this can happen but not to the majority. This is because only very rare individuals could cope with such a massive shift in their consciousness without it creating debilitating mental illness. The shift will be heralded by the generations of the materially dispossessed. These generations will be the harbingers of the shift in consciousness which will bring its own rewards. This will eventually take the form of a kind of material prosperity different to your own. It will be one based on an equality for all. There will be great planetary changes involved. Also, mass movement of people from one part of the globe to another forced in part by global warming. By the end of your century the world will be a radically different one to the one you live on now. It will be the younger generations who bring this change not your own my son. Your generation is primarily a very selfish generation, those following your own are much more considerate and sensitive to the needs of others. This is why already; many changes are occurring which are a reflection on these more sensitive individuals. They are a much gentler people. They find war horrific and will abstain from it. The world is filling quickly in terms of the young, with what your generation would have called conscientious objectors. Their objections are towards killing. Instead they stand for life and saving life. This includes to the best of their ability saving your world. Of course, there are some who will try to follow the old ways of previous generations. They are few in number and will not succeed in causing the havoc, pain and suffering on a global scale. This is their aim and goal. But the divine has other plans, it will not be allowed. The group consciousness of love is far stronger than the group consciousness supporting evil acts towards others, my son. This you will be pleased to hear no doubt. Evidence supporting these words will become more and more clear as time passes. Do not be fearful as you see the old ways and structures crumble and fade away. They will soon die off with those who created them. They served a time, they do not serve this time now occurring. There will be challenges to try to maintain the old, but they will not succeed.

What will be broken down will be rebuilt in a different form. Where there is perceived unity now will become true unity of peoples in your not too distant future. To build a new house where an old one stood first the old must be destroyed, before the new can rise in its place."

S.H. "That is all good to hear. I know that there must be a shift to a higher consciousness for humanity and the rest of the animal kingdom to survive. So, I trust and hope, all of what has been said comes to pass, for the higher good. Also, to eradicate pain and suffering as much as possible. It sounds like a much better world.

One filled with love instead of pain and distrust, which is now so self-evident.

As I go about my day, I do try as best I can to be kind and loving to people in general. Might I also ask how others can best serve to assist in this global shift?"

H.S. "My son, each must follow their hearts, their own intuition. They will know what is right for them. They will each use their own gifts or skills to help others however they feel drawn in their own way. There are many different ways to assist your world heal and improve itself. However, at the bedrock of all activity should lie love. Love is the builder of all. Love should be the force behind all actions wherever possible. If one is not sure then ask yourself, does this action spring from 'love'. If it does and it resonates correctly in your heart. Then go ahead. If not resist the impulse, whatever the reason my son.

Your world is currently being cleansed. Before it can be refilled it needs to be emptied. All that is bad or which does not serve humanity and your planets best interests is being removed. Evil is losing its grip. It is trying to hold on by its fingernails, yet it will not survive. The feminine energies flooding your planet will not resonate with those who do not want to feel it. They will die off.

Do not look to your news media for what is occurring in respect of this truth. You will not find real evidence there. The media, for the most part, represents the old ways, which are crumbling now. These support the interests of a rich minority. Most of whom, though in fairness not all, do not want to see these gentler energies prevail. Where they see peace, they will want war. This is to perpetuate and protect with self-interest the material interests of a few, at the expense of the dispossessed majority.

The creator is the creator of all, not a few. Peace and equality walk hand in hand across your lands now, it will not be defeated my son. The enemy of peace is fear. Where there is fear, there cannot be peace. To fight fear simply allow peace into your hearts. This is not difficult it is a simple choice. Choose peace always. Even within the microcosm of your own life choose peace always. If you are worrying about an ailment you have for example, consciously say to yourself in your own mind, 'I choose peace' and peace will return. Be mindful always of your own thoughts and emotions from moment to moment. If you do, you will know when to keep on choosing peace consciously to return to your own mind. When you do so you will remain in the present moment. This is the point of power. Then and only then are you truly in the presence of God.

Always remember who you are. All of you. That you are love! You are loved! You are all the source of that love! These words once helped you a great deal at a time of great sadness. May these words help and support others in their times of great need also. They are not copy-righted my son. They belong to all, always."

S.H. "Indeed, I agree. Thank you. One of my greatest blessings I would say has been my own faith in God. I have not always had it. For many years when I was much younger I was agnostic in my belief. I struggled then to find inner contentment. Particularly at times of personal struggle. I feel that I have been on a great 'inner journey' seeking out spiritual truth. Having found it I greatly value this inner journey for its riches of spirit which it has brought to my soul. It is I feel, a journey well worth the effort. It is the journey which I most recommend that people make. It requires great courage to face the fears which surface. Meditation has been my greatest tool to achieve this practice. Again, it is one I cannot recommend highly enough to others."

H.S. "Indeed, the journey of which you speak has been a remarkable one. It has been remarkable simply because you chose to make it. So, many do not. You have not feared change as much as you once thought. You have been through many subtle shifts in character and emotion. Only your own soul is witness to this. Not even your parents. This is true for many. The purpose of life is to make a similar journey. This journey is one which takes you back to your source. It is yours and everyone else's birth right. To discover and know the essence of their true beingness which is of God, which is of love and awareness. You are each the embodiment of this. These words are but one of many means to spark alight that same inner knowing in the many in the world, who are trying to find and discover what lies behind the emptiness that they might feel. With these words and with this knowledge such emptiness can be replaced and banished. Between these words a feeling or emotion that the reader feels, speaks silently to their soul. It strokes and awakens within themselves a slumbering remembrance of the truthfulness of these words. If so and another soul finds themselves awakened, where once they were asleep, then they can rejoice in their awakening to who they truly are. Who they truly always were. Then may the light sparkle more strongly through their eyes and may the love that they radiate more purposefully go out into the world to help with greater awakenings still."

S.H. "Yes, I do remember some of the earliest teachings I read about spirituality. What struck me most was not the content of the words. But, how an awakening to a truth which had been hidden somehow occurred on the wave of an emotion. Rather than a wave of thoughts in my mind. I 'felt' the truth of the words rather than just intellectually assimilating them. They instilled an awakening in my heart rather than in my mind. Some say the seat of the soul in the human body is in the heart. Is that correct?"

H.S. "Yes my son, the souls anchor to the body is the heart chakra. That is why sometimes a 'broken heart' on an emotional level can lead to a loss of life. Although at the highest level the soul in question has chosen to leave their body at that time. The heart is therefore the true seat of knowing not the mind. It is the contact to each person's own highest wisdom. So, listen do not ignore it. Your conscience, speaks to you for good purpose and good reason. It helps you all stay on a true path. All you need to do is to listen and follow, my son."

S.H. "So, is this the key part. The key method to gain entry to that, which is the title of this book, i.e. "Awakening to Love'."

H.S. "Yes, it is part of the remembering. This I say because you have always known the way. You have just forgotten. It is awakening to what you have always known deep inside. This is the same for each of you, who choose this under taking. The seekers of the truth."

S.H. "Okay."

S.H. "I am wondering, with this shift in human consciousness currently happening, what its impact might be on other aspects of human behaviour.

I have noticed that in my own country the United Kingdom, that there has been a big increase in people adopting a vegan diet and lifestyle so to speak. This does not surprise me. I myself am moving towards such with my diet. Can you comment please on the eating of animal products?"

H.S. "A vegan diet is the best way to go, not just for the health of your own selves but also for the health and welfare of animals and your own environment. It is quite simple. Irrespective of the ethics of the question. Your own experience of different animal products on your health and the scientific findings in general prove this to be the case, no question.

You do not need to eat any of it and neither do humans in general. Again, the vested business interests across the country are trying to abate the change. Yet change will continue to grow and spread as human consciousness grows and awakens towards not just greater compassion towards the animal kingdom but kindness towards your own selves in terms of how you harm your own bodies with animal products, including their meat of course.

A society which does not eat meat is the first sign that they are of a higher consciousness than those who do eat meat and animal products. This is and should be no surprise.

When you stop eating such produce your vibration will quickly change to a higher frequency. The thought and emotions of the individual change in many beneficial and positive ways. The happiness levels of the individual increases as well as the energy levels of such individuals.

This big step is part of the evolutionary cycle of any society. In turn part of this shift is the refusal to kill other human beings in any sort of conflict. This is a directly related matter. A reflection of the same level of growth in human consciousness. All of the animal kingdom share the same consciousness and awareness as human beings."

S.H. "Surely then plants are also conscious, is it not wrong also to eat plants. Obviously, this would be a bit of a problem if it was also, not right?"

H.S. "This is not a matter of right or wrong. It is a matter of what is acceptable to the divine. Plants exist for a variety of reasons. All creatures with a few exceptions live on plants or their prey does. Some creatures of course eat other creatures to exist. On a conscious level these creatures have no other choice in terms of their survival. Humanity does. When you live from the consciousness of love, certain activities fall away out of compassion for the greater whole of which you are all a part. By choosing to live with greater compassion to the rest of nature. To not harm nature wherever possible this is a marker of an awakening to the higher consciousness of which you all truly are my son.

If the lands used for the breeding of animals for consumption were to be used instead for crops, famine on your planet would stop.

When this happens, your society will have completed a cycle. It will have arrived in a new age of true equality and compassion. This will happen when all those who run your societies have reached this higher level of conscious awakening to love."

S.H. "Could you please define exactly what consciousness is please?"

H.S. "Consciousness is a flow, an unlimited supply of love. Think of a river. It begins in the sky falling as rain. The river flows to the sea and returns in part to the atmosphere. The cycle continues. Love is like this its supply is eternal. It is cyclical. It flows from all to all in a continuous cycle. It is unlimited, everlasting or omniscient, omnipresent and omnipotent. All powerful, yes, it is. Within this flow of love all is contained. Nothing is outside of it. Therefore, awareness and intelligence is also contained within it. All memories that have ever been, of all experiences are contained within it like a giant computer, which can never crash.

So, this flow of loving awareness of which you are simultaneously part of but also its entirety, is who you and 'all that is,' are. You are that.

Once again, to use the analogy of the fish asking, 'where is this ocean that I keep hearing about', so often it is with humanity enquiring about 'God' or the unity of consciousness."

S.H. "What strikes me is how something which most would think to be such a complex thing, can be described in so few words."

H.S. "It has been described at the simplest level for it to be easily understood by many.

Your words my son are one dimensional, for certain things your words fail to describe. How can you have a word for something most cannot explain? Most people would find love difficult to describe in more than a few words, yet most appreciate how fundamental to their being and existence that it is. Do they not?"

S.H. "Yes, indeed. So, consciousness is fundamentally who we are then?"

H.S. "Yes, but you are all expressions of it too. Your projection of it, is not just your physical form but all that is. You and all are that which is the unity of consciousness shared."

S.H. "I would be interested to know, whether even if consciousness itself is omnipresent, whether the vibration or level of human consciousness is different, say to, two thousand years ago, around the time of Christ?"

H.S. "My son the vibration was not so different on the planet then itself my son. The difference you would notice, were you able to visit at that time would be more about the consciousness in general of humanity incarnated at that time. They were less evolved in a spiritual sense. There were however, pockets of individuals who were very open to the ways of the spirit. That was a time of Christ's brief lifetime on Earth in human form.

At that time, it heralded a shift in consciousness of humanity similar to your own time. However, the shift was very small compared to the time you find yourself in now. This is reflected in the vast number of human beings living on Earth at this, your time. Their own souls are aware of the opportunities for soul growth at this time of great shift. The numbers of persons incarnate adds to the power for consciousness to rise, at this your time. This is due to the collective human consciousness being greater due to the numbers.

Do not concern yourself my son however, with the violent and destructive incidents which are still occurring in different parts of your planet. These are final gasps of an old consciousness, a remaining few are holding onto. Evil cannot prevail in a climate of love. As the enlightened consciousness grows with each new already previously enlightened soul setting foot on the soil of your Earth the grip of evil will diminish and fade. The opposite may appear to be the case. This is the fault of your media keeping the focus on negativity and fear instead of beauty and peace which is most prevalent all around your planet. In the nearness of time as the consciousness rises further the focus for your media will be on positive change. Keep your focus on goodness and kindness in the world my son. It is all around you all, know in your heart of hearts that the full force and power of the almighty is guiding those whose hearts and minds resonate in and with love."

S.H. "Once we have woken up to our true nature, i.e. the spirit within us and what that represents. Then is it possible to go back to the part unconscious state that we hold prior to such an awakening?"

H.S. "My son you cannot forget once you have woken up to that understanding. You can however, choose to ignore it and revert to ways of old if you so wish. However, your conscience which you also have woken up to more, will be a constant prompt to bring you back to a truer path. To be present as much of your time as possible, takes a form of self-discipline, if to be present as much as possible is what you seek my son. It involves keeping your mind, body and emotions in the best health possible, to enable the optimum clarity that spirit can work through. This should not be a struggle, so as to hinder your own progress and flow. You do not need to struggle to be that which you already are, for you are that. You are consciousness in embodiment."

S.H. "I remember during my own long process in trying to awaken to something deeper inside myself, when I was early on my path. It felt like peeling away layers of an onion. It is quite a slow process I found. Sometimes it felt like some of the layers I peeled away from my being were more like a crusty shell, on an emotional level. Perhaps this was my awareness that they were old emotions, which had been present for a long time."

H.S. "Yes, indeed. People all have their own different experiences of course. What is important for anyone's growth is reaching the freedom of shedding that which prevents growth towards an individual's own greater awareness of who they are. The true nature of their own spiritual nature. To reach this often means shedding a lifetimes worth of erroneous belief systems and negative self-judgement. All of which creates inner barriers to growth and personal joy. Self-love will come when such emotions are shed and released. These negative emotions are barriers to good health and if left unattended they can lead to numerous illnesses which only make your own evolvement more difficult still."

S.H. "Can the many numerous forms of healing therapies help with shifting the numerous blockages which can impede our growth to awakening and greater well-being?"

H.S. "Yes, of course my son. Follow the 'inner teacher', the intuition, to guide you the right one for each of you. If you ask they will come. Healers come in many forms. They can help to guide spiritual energy to help heal much whether physical, mental or emotional. However, all illness fundamentally begins at the emotional/mental level and progresses outwards into physical manifestation. The thoughts you hold either create wellness or ill health through their effect on the immune system. The more love centred you can be, the more your thought will follow a positive track and the better your health will be."

S.H. "As we are talking about health here and already accepting the idea or belief that the more open we are towards loving ourselves and others, which will help us to stay healthy. I am curious to ask another question about further detail on the effects on health, regarding a person's diet and about further implications around eating animals and animal products, even though we touched on this earlier in our dialogue."

H.S. "Yes, my son animal products do not resonate with your own body's vibration. As your own vibration changes the metabolism of your body changes. Just as the metabolism of the body slows generally as the body ages. The opposite occurs, as the vibration of the body is raised through raised consciousness and higher levels of spiritual awareness or knowledge. This is why younger yet more evolved members of humanity are shifting to a plant based diet. An animal based diet is denser. It is more difficult to digest. It influences the mental/emotional state of being. It will not surprise you to know that to eat the flesh of an animal includes not just ingesting whatever that their body's have absorbed, but the emotions of that animal. The emotions are held in the physical cells of the animal's bodies generally in the forms of disease or 'dis-ease' because of the pain and trauma they have experienced in their often short lifetimes. The vibration of this is passed on to the person who consumes the animal. Emotions have a life of their own. This is how emotions can get trapped in the body and need to be released to prevent illness forming in the places these emotions can be held in the emotional body.

Energetically this is transferred to the corresponding place in the physical body. When the emotion is held around the heart centre, or chakra, such as a painful emotion or sadness, it can also over time if not healed affect the physical heart. Such is the case for most of the corresponding organs of the body. This of course reflecting wherever such an emotional pain is held.

If You consume a plant based diet there will be no such effect on the body if the source of such is organic. Plants do not store emotional pain in this way. They are aware but not sentient to the same degree. They do not have a nervous system. Neither physically or emotionally. Put simply, plants do not get anxious. Members of the animal family and insect family can worry. Proof of this my son is that certain insects will sting if threatened!"

six

Finding Your Way to Love

S.H. "I have found the most difficult obstacle to feeling peace within, is the emotion of fear. How can I best overcome my fears?"

H.S. "By facing them. By facing them individually, as they arise."

S.H. "A lot of people struggle to face their fears, I think because to do so, often brings up anxiety around their fears and this makes facing them more difficult."

H.S. "Yes indeed. Take one particular fear, such as health anxiety. Especially in older people this is a common anxiety. They fear pain, disability and death which could result from illness. Often illnesses are indeed born of their anxiety. The auto-immune system is suppressed by their anxiety. Many people are aware that this is the case, so they then worry about the worrying they do. So how do you stop a cycle such as this?

You stop it in part through mindfulness. Being aware of the thoughts in your mind. Watching them and so changing them to something different, when you notice yourself worrying. In the case of anxiety about an illness, it helps to trust in the intelligence inherent within your own body. Many think at the first sign of illness that they should visit their doctor. This being born out of worry about what the symptom might indicate.

What they so often forget is that the inherent consciousness of the body itself is already and constantly working to heal itself. The body is in a constant state of change and repair. That is its nature. It knows what to do at any given time to self-repair. Trust in your body it is a remarkable God given creation. Allow your doctors to assist your healing of course when required but the body's inbuilt doctor is always on hand."

S.H. "Thank you. I return to this writing project after a long winter break.

So how do we 'find our way to love'?

I think it is something most of us crave a lot of the time, for one reason or another. For me personally, I think I crave it a great deal, in part because I believe that my own mother found it very difficult to show her love to me in a nurturing way when I was very young child. I think that ultimately, I have been seeking that deep maternal love which I never received to the degree I needed to feel secure in myself, from other women as a result throughout my adult life. This has proved to be unobtainable in my experience and perhaps, not to have been unexpected."

H.S. "My son, welcome back indeed to this process.

You speak of a need deeply held, in the core of your being, a memory of lack as you see it, which has stuck with you, though you have only been conscious of the reasons for it in more recent times. You are correct in your perception and you know that such love was never intended to be withheld to cause you any suffering. Your own mother had her own issues to overcome to show you the love which you instinctively sought as a baby and a young child. Your sister being born soon after and all of which that entailed, as you know.

However, let's just say that you not only survived to tell the tale so to speak, but through your own experience you have sought out love, not just from others but within your own self and soul for your own self-expression and self-nurture. You have awoken to the reality of the constant river of love within your own self, which is inherent in all beings.

You do not need to seek outside of yourself, the love you so crave. When you need that nurture go within to find it and once you have reconnected with that love, share it and spread it with all around you, by helping and being kind to others, however you can.

The energy which vitalises your own body is the energy of life. Yes, you may need food for sustenance also, but it is the same love which supplies that to you. Consciousness within creation is love. Love is also consciousness. That is what you all are my son."

S.H. "Okay, I have already reached this point of believing this to be true. How, though do the many people who do not yet believe that they are love in embodied form realise that is who they truly are, come to know and believe such?"

H.S. "My son by going within. By reading books such as this one. By asking their own soul for the answers to life's mysteries. By seeking, by constantly seeking truth my son. That is the way. By following their own instincts and intuition 'the inner teacher' to wherever or whoever it leads them too. Nothing happens by coincidence. They must learn to watch and learn from the divine signs and synchronicities which come into their own life. As they are guided on their own different paths they will find that it is always guiding them to the discovery of who they truly are. This being love, light and wisdom. Unity with the one divine mother/father God of which they are all part. This may seem too grand, too big an idea to comprehend, yet they are here now in this life! They are a part of the universe. They think their own embodiment is their own limitation. It is the opposite. Your bodies are more like the sockets plugged into the matrix of the universe. The physical points of connection to the unity of all that is, in the physical realm. In the spiritual realm, it is similar but the connection is a mental one more than physical. In the spiritual one, your mind is more easily connected to the divine mind. In some respects, it is easier to become more aware of the divine in the physical world but only after the process of 'awakening' to such. Do you see?"

S.H. "Yes, I do. I think we both would agree that one of the biggest blockages we all create to feeling love is instead focusing on problems which only lead us to worry and fear. They take us from the moment so that we are not present in the present moment. This means that we are less likely to be open and feeling love within. Correct?"

H.S. "Yes, bravo, correct my son. You don't need me! Indeed, you yourself have said it. Worry is futile and energy wasted, it leads to dis-ease of all sorts. However, as you have discovered in your own life my son, it can be more difficult than you might think. It requires constant awareness of your own thoughts and feelings and developing the ability to change them at will to thoughts that are more positive and peaceful."

S.H. "I am back writing again after nearly six weeks of injury to my left arm from a trapped nerve. I enjoyed the time away from writing this book. Not because I don't enjoy the process of being creative, but because we have had some nice weather and I prefer to be outdoors (most of this writing has been done indoors with a pot of tea for company in a very old but lovely hotel in my home seaside town).

My pain has very much eased, so I am back online with my writing. Any advice or suggestions please?

I do believe that we are awakening to love or something similar? Ha, ha......"

H.S. "My son you must be feeling better and your sense of humour has returned. Always a good sign!

There is no rush with this project. Take your time. Enjoy it as much as possible."

S.H. "I have not been able to meditate either for six weeks, which I have found frustrating. So, I suppose a part of me is raring to go to get back online with this project. So, where were we?"

H.S. "Indeed we were talking about loving ourselves, in particular the parts of our body or character which is not pleasing to ourselves or another. Our tendency, to judge others and ourselves. As regards others, indeed you never know their story or what their life has entailed unless you know them well. You do not know what has led to their own struggles or difficulties in life. Hence patience and compassion should always be shown to them, my son. Irrespective of what has gone before, for others there is always chance and time for change. Change can come in a moment. All that is required is the desire and decision to change. Whatever the change of direction of the individual. This could be in thought, behaviour or action. My son there is a saying, 'you reap what you sow,' this occurs on many levels my son. It involves not just physically but also people's behaviour and attitude towards you, or others, dependent on how you have been treating those others, which your life has brought you into contact with. Wish for others what you would wish for yourself. Treat others, how you would wish to be treated. This is always the way to proceed in life. If you yearn for peace and happiness in your own life bring it INTO THE LIFE OF OTHERS.

It has been noticed my son that you have been yearning for peace more than usual in your own life. You have been noticing bird song more than usual. This has been brought to you as a gift by the creator more than usual in your environment. Through the love of the creator to help your own recovery my son."

S.H. "Thank you so much. You have made me feel quite emotional. It has been a difficult time for me again recently. As time goes by I notice more and more how I suffer at times with anxiety and often find myself worrying about some ailment or other, which makes me feel rather self-indulgent at times. This being a part of my character I don't like. Any suggestions on how a person can break this tendency towards anxiety and worry?"

H.S. "When there is peace there is balance. When there is balance, there is peace. When there is balance mentally, emotionally, there is physical health. As you have discovered my son. There is a link between them all: PEACE-BALANCE-HEALTH or HEALTH-PEACE-BALANCE.

Peace comes first. This leads to balance. Health results.

You were not at peace worrying about a medical test result or outcome. Tension threw you out of balance and illness resulted. You ended up with a trapped nerve causing pain in your left arm. Your challenge then was to surrender your pain and be patient to allow the healing to occur. As a therapy, you used your garden, by spending more time sitting outside. You focused on the beauty of your surroundings, including the bird song, to bring you peace and rest. This ultimately allowed you to recover your health sufficiently to continue with your usual activity. Be it exercise, meditation or this writing process. These activities help your peace of mind, as that is what you enjoy most my son. Such is life. The lesson here for you, was no matter how difficult, was letting go of such things, until you recovered enough to resume them. Such as sleeping positions, cycling positions or meditation positions.

By letting go, you allowed your body to relax enough to heal through relaxation."

S.H. "Thank you. It sounds quite simple. But surrendering to the disability, be it temporary can be so difficult. Then the discomfort just continues. But I sense here the necessity of a bigger letting go. A letting go of the fear which causes the pattern of the nature of my personal worries.

I remember when I was younger my focus was more positive about my health and well-being. Not the fear of sickness, injury and ailments. I need to let go of this fear which just perpetuates this ill-health loop. I see that I need to focus on being healthy. Instead of focusing on being unwell. What we focus on we create. If we focus on wellness. We will create wellness. If we focus on ailments or ill-health then that is what we will create."

H.S. "Yes, bravo my son. Well said. Well done. Shift your focus to health and wellness. Say each day, 'I am well, I am healthy'. Be grateful. Focus on all those parts of your body each day which are working as they should be. In doing so you will keep on helping and healing those which are not. Then you are being <u>health conscious not sickness conscious.</u> You are focusing on health. Not illness. Your habit has been to keep focusing each day on what is wrong with you instead of what is right with you. Shift the habit, shift the focus to being positive each and every day about your wellness. Mental or physical. Instead of focusing on the stress, focus on the peace. It is all about where the focus lies."

S.H. "I am healthy. I am well. Thank you."

S.H. "Today it is raining and I am struggling to come up with a question. Can you help please, Higher-Self?"

H.S. "My son welcome back again. You are feeling better. You are feeling well and more aligned both physically and mentally. You have let go of your fear of illness, for now. We say for now, not to be negative, because you know this is a challenge for you, not to worry.

Worry is a challenge for most people. Some more so than for others. We would like to talk here a bit more about the subject of worry.

What is worry? Well it is a mental process is it not?

Usually it revolves around a fear of loss. Whether it be health related. Money related. Relationship related. Family related. It is most often a fear of losing something that we hold dear in our lives. Something to which we have become attached. Whether it be a physical object such as a house or a car or a person who is special to us such as a son, daughter or spouse. It is through our attachment that gives rise to a fear of loss of such things.

Where does the attachment come from?

Usually, it is again a fear of lack of such material objects, including a fear of a lack of money or the fear of the loss of the love of another.

The attachment is based on the presumption of lack. That the universe cannot provide the love we get from another, or the fear that the universe is finite in its generosity of provision to us, be it food that we need or the money to buy the things that we may want or need.

However, this fear of lack or loss is also based in and on a lack of trust in the universe and the compassion which the creator holds all within. For all that comes to you, which sustains and nurtures you, whether it be food, water, shelter or love comes from the creator. Yet the creator resides within you. Therefore, you cannot be outside of these things.

When you focus on the lack of them. Then that is what the mind brings to your experience. You experience your reality through your own beliefs. By this we mean that this is how you create your own reality. Therefore, if your thoughts dwell in abundance. Be it health, wealth or love then this is what you will experience for yourself and those closest to you. Focus on health. Focus on wealth, if that is what you wish for.

Focus on love for yourself and towards others and that will be your experience. That is what the universe will manifest for you and your experience. That is simply how the universe works. Mind is the builder. Use your minds to build through your focus, that which you want to create. If you want peace, focus on peace my son."

S.H. "We all yearn for peace in our lives, be it our personal lives or in our communities and of course we wish for peace in our world. I understand that we must begin with ourselves. As the saying goes, 'when there is peace in ourselves, there will be peace in our family. When there is peace in our families, there will be peace in our communities. When there is peace in our communities, there will be peace in our countries and when there is peace in all our countries there will be peace in the world'.

Using this analogy therefore perhaps, we could put forward the proposition that peace in the world begins in the mind of each individual. This makes peace in the world a simple choice, of always choosing and so always coming back to peace in our own minds?"

H.S. "Yes indeed my son and well put. That is exactly so, where else could peace originate.

Let's imagine your world being hit by an asteroid. If big enough this could cause a lot of chaos and concern. If, however all affected choose peace and calm all will be well. If, however the opposite is the reaction chaos is likely to ensue. Choose peace always. Also, as we have stated previously here, when you choose peace you will be in the present moment in your minds. Your awareness will be fixed in the present moment and your own inner teacher i.e. the intuition will guide you, each and every one to the wisest decision available to you to overcome whatever the problem you are facing. You will have the divine wisdom arise within and guide your decision through the process. This also applies of course to your everyday concerns for each and every one, if you will but listen to the inner promptings of your true being. Listen to the still small voice within, be guided by the hand of your 'conscience'.

You have been enjoying watching the swifts fly above you this day. My son, their navigation skills come from the creator. They listen and follow their inner knowing as to which direction in which to fly, to take them to their intended destination. So, it should be, for human beings if they wish to be in the right place, be it physically or mentally."

S.H. "I have been trying to avoid drinking any alcohol to help my health and to maintain and strengthen my own connection with God. Can you please comment on this? The three times this year when I have drunk a small amount of alcohol I have regretted doing so, as I wish to maintain my awareness of the present moment to the highest degree possible. I have noticed that although alcohol can have a relaxing effect, ultimately it diminishes my clarity and level of awareness."

H.S. "My son this is exactly so and for all humans. It is a method of escape like most drugs my son. It is harmful to the body even in small doses, if they are repeated often enough. The body must work hard to rid itself of the chemical which it is. It blocks the impulses in the brain. The neural pathways are temporarily switched off. The connection with spirit is also dulled by the effect of the alcohol chemical on the brain and body. All the workings of the body are slowed. Alcohol is not good for the body. In fact, it is a poison. As you know if you consume too much of it in a short period of time it will lead to death of the physical body."

seven

Love is the Key

S.H. "What is the purpose of life here on earth?"

H.S. "What is the purpose of life anywhere?

Life is a divinely inspired existence. Irrespective of the form in which the life finds itself, it is an experience for the creator. Life is the creator experiencing life in all its forms imaginable. In the physical realm, life is a multitude of choices. The more evolved the creature in its physical form, the more aware and evolved is its spirit within and without. We say this as it is the life force which holds each form together while in the physical realm. Life has no more purpose than it simply is such. You are here as part of the experience of the creator, experiencing life in one of the many myriad forms of physical embodiment experienced. You each have free will to choose as you please your experiences on earth. Through the soul's evolution your experiences will be reflective of the level of consciousness you all hold at the time. The higher the consciousness in question the deeper the degree of love and compassion shown to those around you, the deeper the spiritual wisdom accessible to the individual, the more in tune with the creator that individual will be. This will be reflected in the actions and choices of the individual in each moment. The higher the awareness of the individual then the more the consciousness of those around will be raised.

Consciousness is most pervasive, it ebbs and flows like the tide, at different times. One individual operating from a consciousness of a high level can have a very big effect on the human group consciousness. Take Jesus, who walked your earth about two thousand years ago. The effect of his consciousness is still being felt today around your world. His work has left a legacy of predominantly good will towards others. Only man's changing of his message at times, has had any negative impact. This was never his desire of course. His message was to love and help all people in a way each would like to be helped and supported in times of need.

Many individuals, past and present have played a role in raising human consciousness. At this time humanity is going through an enormous shift in consciousness globally. The intention of the shift has been to raise the awareness of human beings to their true divine nature. In much the same way, you are endeavouring such with this book. Your efforts are heart felt and loving. Your message here is to show and tell others that they are not the body, they are not the mind. They are each a form of embodiment for divine loving consciousness. That is who you are. That is your reason and purpose for being here now. To embody and share divine loving consciousness with your fellow man. Now and each day that you are alive on this earth."

S.H. "So many people, it seems are just not just only unaware of these truths, but also sadly seem to have little interest in them. How can these words, or this type of message reach these people?"

H.S. "My son, all will seek when they are ready to seek. Each individual is at a different stage in their own evolution. Most will seek their own answers to life and existence when trouble comes knocking at their own door. It is in times of distress and pain that an opening occurs. When their own mental anguish and suffering triggers within them the longing, which is mostly silenced, due to their own usual and everyday concerns silencing their still small voice within. There are so many distractions in your modern world. These distractions and a fear of appearing different to others also prevents many searching or expressing their own deeply held spiritual beliefs. Most people do not like to stand out from the crowd or to appear to be too different for fear of ridicule by their peers. Some like yourself my son, are prepared to step over the threshold of belief and follow the calling of their own soul. It is not the destiny of all souls to assist others with their spiritual growth. However, this is indeed a large part of your own calling. To help ease the pain and suffering of others. You have learnt the hard way that unless your heart remains open then your true connection to divine inspiration is closed to you. So, it is also with others. The wisdom of the heart exceeds many fold the wisdom of the mind. The mind is like a computer not plugged into its power source if it is not engaged with divine wisdom. Love is the source of this connection. All it takes is an open heart. To keep an open heart my son, involves constant forgiveness and non-judgement towards others. This is not easy for many. The mind and your thoughts consistently for many, preclude the above from happening. When you are judging another in a negative way or holding resentment towards others you are not able to be compassionate to those others and your love will not flow.

Let go of your prejudices. Let go of the perceived hurt caused by others towards you. Let go of your worries and fears for yours and your future generations. Trust that they will be held safe in the loving hands of the mother father God who loves them all equally in each moment."

S.H. "Since our last conversation, a few days ago there has been a terrible bombing in Manchester, in the United Kingdom, where I live. This was for me, too distressing to engage with. I switched off the media sources close to me to avoid hearing the details.

Much pain and suffering is of course the result of such hateful actions. I can barely think about the pain many will have to endure as a result. This is happening in many parts of the world. I know that previous decisions and actions by our government over recent years are partly to blame for bringing such troubles on to the shores of my country. What can be done to help this situation?"

H.S. "My son, this is an open-ended question. Yet there is a simple answer. To love all and serve all. This applies to all humans. Love and forgiveness is the only way. Hate breeds hate. Violence begets violence. It is not a complicated answer at its core. The complications only come in the strategy of dealing with these threats of violence and their action when they occur. However, I know this is not the answer you seek here. Love and compassion is the only route to soften the hearts and minds of those intent on following a twisted ideology of using such violence towards others. This is not the way of God. It is the way of fear and revenge invested in the twisted logic of the minds of those who have been taught false truths. They have been indoctrinated in the ways of violence to satisfy the false ideology of others. We say false, because it is simply not based on universal truths. The main one being that God embodies all creation, therefore all human beings too, irrespective of race, colour or creed. Teach the loving ways of peace always my son. Radiate your peace, light and beauty to others, so that they may see it in themselves also. This is the only way to heal your world. Those intent on purveying their own ways of violence and killing are small in number. The waves of love, of the majority, will in time drown and engulf their soul's, only those who transform to the ways of peace will be able to survive these changes. To some degree the upsurge in this type of violence is their own resistance to the change which they do not like and resent. At the deepest level, they have a fear of love, due to their own self-loathing in most cases. In their heart of hearts and their own conscience, sits itself uncomfortably upon their own shoulders. This preventing peace from entering their own existence of being. They can only feel comfortable surrounding themselves with like-minded individuals. Yet they are too few in number. The earth now is populated by a great number of wise, kind and benevolent souls such as yourself, intent on doing good only, helping others along the way. Return always to the divinity within yourselves time and time again. Until eventually in time that becomes your constant awareness. Awaken once and for all to the love inherent within all being."

S.H. "Thank you."

S.H. "Since my last question, we have had a holiday break and in the interval another terrorist attack, in a part of London, which I visited only a few days before the incident. I am now back in my home town. A place of relative peace and tranquillity beside the sea. I count myself fortunate to be living here away from the greater risk of danger, which places like London sadly provide at this present time. Had my destiny been different, I could have been visiting Camden market with my son as we did at the time the atrocious attack occurred, rather than a few days earlier. How much does fate or destiny play a part in such occurrences?"

H.S. "My son. Your destiny is yours. The destiny of others is theirs. Each create their own destiny over the course of time. In part, due to the previous behaviour of their own and in part that of others. The time of death of an individual is not predestined. It is chosen by the individual at the highest level. This might sound strange or illogical to your own, or to the minds of others. A soul cannot set itself free from the bondage of human mortality without choosing to do so. The reason for this is simple. How can a soul shed its body unless pre-ordained?

For a soul to be released from life there must be an agreement between the soul and its own Higher-Self or higher aspect of being. The connection with God at this level is all knowing. However, the ordinary level of consciousness of the soul in question is unaware of the immediate future in the very most cases. This is not to imply the complicity of the Higher-Self and the one causing the death to occur if by force and seemingly without agreement. The soul experiencing the death of the body has made the sacrifice to spare those others who have not chosen at the deepest level to cease their own human lifetime. Therefore, even in an event of seemingly great random chaos, there is a kind of order beneath the surface. All human beings are like actors suffering from seeming amnesia as to their true nature of being divinity in human form connected to all beings and all life. The experience of the pain and suffering by those involved will in time raise their own consciousness through such. In the same way that sugar is released from the sugar cane by the beating with the stick. So, the pain and suffering of all in time brings to the surface the sweetness of their own being. To in turn be demonstrated towards others and self."

S.H. "Many people I think would struggle with such a suggestion that they have agreed to their own death for the benefit of others. To save others from a premature death that their soul is not yet ready for. I think, many would also find this difficult to understand logically."

H.S. "That may be so, my son. Yet this is the order of things. It is expressed through the love of one soul to another to further the chance of greater growth for the soul who has chosen to stay. All the while unaware that the other souls have chosen to make the sacrifice so that others might live instead themselves. This is at times shown in a more obvious way when a mother or father puts themselves in harm's way to protect their child. It is the same principle of behaviour performed in a more obvious or transparent manner. It is an action of love no less than the aforementioned one performed at a sub-conscious level.

So, your own fate for each of you lies in your own hands. At the deepest level the time of your own death is your own choosing.

Though in most cases this is not consciously known by the individual."

S.H. "We have just had a general election in my country, the United Kingdom. The result was most unexpected by many in the country. It drew to my attention to the fact, that within our politics, there is a sense of a tribal attitude and tendency regarding the behaviour by many people. Looking at this and I believe it to be a reflection of the consciousness of the population, many politicians in our country, treat the population as their servants rather than the other way around, as I believe it should be. This is the case, in some of what I believe to be more successful economies, such as that of Switzerland. With greater humility and compassion towards others, I believe this could change. If everyone could live from a place of trust and love according to their own inherent gifts. I believe, we could live in a society where money was no longer required. A world where each person followed their own calling and we produced much as we do now. We could obtain and share all things for free. Each person living from a place of selflessness taking and using only what they need.

A world in which greed had evaporated from the minds and hearts of all beings. This might seem a utopian world view of sorts. Yet, it does not deny the possibility of such a world existing does it."

H.S. "My son your view of the world as it could be, is a possible scenario, which one day could be realised on your Earth. Yes, the consciousness of all still needs to raise somewhat still. This however, is being worked on by the beings of the higher realms. Indeed, this type of society does exist in different worlds. On other planets, far away, who are much more advanced than your own. This is in terms of both time and consciousness. Such beings are indeed more highly evolved than your own and have learned through much pain and experience that this way of living is not only possible but preferable.

By living this way your provisions both on a planetary and an individual basis are sustainable. The resources of your planet are finite. When the populations of your world live in such a way personal satisfaction and happiness is encouraged. The consideration of others is paramount and all are viewed as one family. The realization that all are part of one consciousness, one being only, at the deepest level. You are in truth the awareness and energy that you all are. You are not the body. The body fails and dies. You are not the mind. The mind is like your reflection in the mirror. The inner beholder is who you are, the energy and loving awareness of the beholder. You all are, the loving awareness that animates all forms of life and being throughout your world, universe and beyond."

S.H. "I was also told by an Indian Avatar once, that we are not the body, but consciousness."

H.S. "Yes my son that is correct. You are however more than just conscious awareness. You are also at the grandest level all that consciousness pervades. Which is in turn all of creation. You are divinity manifest in human form. That divinity shines from your eyes my son. Let your light shine my son. Let it ignite within others the conscious awareness within them also. So, play your part, in a grand awakening of the creator in human form. The next stage of consciousness is the creator working with humanity, conscious of its true source and nature, co-creating a better world for all. This will eventually stretch out beyond your world in the distant future. You are like a seed my son of a much greater expansion of the qualities inherent within all humanity. Love and compassion for others will encircle your globe, sooner than you think possible."

S.H. "Many people died in a terrible fire in a block of flats yesterday (as I write) in London. The scene was reminiscent of the nine-eleven disaster in New York in 2001. London has taken a pummelling in recent weeks in terms of disasters and violent incidents of man against man. Is there something greater going on beyond the mundane likelihood of pure chance?"

H.S. "My son, the occurrences of which you speak were largely pre-planned. The fire was indeed a disaster waiting to happen. It was <u>not</u> intentional but arose due to a combination of factors. High rise buildings are inherently dangerous by design. They are obviously unsafe in the event of a fire. In cities, they are often domiciled by poor people to save money on land costs for housing. If you choose to live in a high rise building you are taking a risk with fire. Buildings need to be designed with greater thought of people's safety. Sadly, for this building it was not paramount. It should never have been built as it was my son. The occupants would have had a sense of foreboding for many years if resident there of what was to come.

Human beings need to feel a sense of being one with nature to result in a healthy emotional state. To live, each on top of one another results in those above not being connected to the ground, at a deep level. This sense of not feeling rooted to a place gives the individual a sense of insecurity in their surroundings. When one lives at ground level there is a greater harmony in the being, compared to the one who chooses to live above the ground. In the same way, those who choose to live in nature rather than in a city will mostly feel more at harmony within themselves."

S.H. "I have a tendency towards judging others often based on first appearances. Sometimes I am right, at other times wrong. I do not think this is an attractive quality to have in myself. Could you comment on this please?"

H.S. "My son, who or what are you judging here?

As regards an individual, any individual in fact. If you do not know them personally, then what is your judgment based upon? It is based on your own experience and memory of others and your own interactions, or lack of such with them. Your tendency my son is to remember the negative experiences with some people who do not resonate with your own self. Those who do not resonate with your own energy are the ones you tend to find the most different from yourself and therefore the reason why you are not drawn to those individuals. If you instinctively feel that their lifestyle is very different to your own you make the judgement that because they choose to practice another lifestyle to your own, then you would not be in harmony with them in a social circumstance. Once you have this idea about them a barrier is erected between themselves and yourself. This then tends to cloud your judgement which prevents further interaction. If you can set any prior judgement aside and allow the inner being through. The inner beauty that all possess in differing degrees you will allow a change of heart and mind to occur. You allow the humanity to come through, thereby allowing a shift in your attitude and allowing the initial ideas and thoughts to shift and change through compassion and non-judgement. When you do this, you are then indeed practicing non-judgement allowing their light to shine."

S.H. "I would like to ask about the human trait of competitiveness in an individual. Today, I was sitting in a service at my daughter's primary school, where certificates were handed out to some children, but not to all, for their achievements. On the one hand, I believe this is a positive thing. On the other hand, some children very seldom receive one. I would suspect from this that many of the latter could start to feel like a failure, from an early stage in their lives?"

H.S. "My son the inference in your question is that competition between others is or can be bad. Is that what you are asking?"

S.H. "No. In certain circumstances I question its wisdom. I do not like to think of some children, at such a young age, think that they are failures. When so much of their lives are still ahead of them."

H.S. "My son, I see. What is the purpose of competition firstly?
Is it not to produce a winner?
If so then by definition, there must also be losers.
However, here you are I believe talking of recognition of what the children have learned through their own progress. Then being recognised for such. Is this correct?"

S.H. "Yes. Correct."

H.S. "In which case this is a good thing. Not a bad one.
It will encourage all to do their best in their studies."

S.H. "I myself struggle, when I come up against the parents, who I feel are particularly competitive and put that on their child to encourage them to be likewise. I do not find this quality attractive."

H.S. "Why do you not like it my son?"

S.H. "Because I myself do not like to feel like a loser."

H.S. "A loser compared to whom?"

S.H. "Others who I might perceive to have been more successful in life than myself."

H.S. "Does this come from envy or jealousy towards others or from your own self-judgement about having the idea that you could have done better in life to date?"

S.H. "The latter."

H.S. "So, it comes from self-judgement not judgement by others."

S.H. "Yes, self-judgement."

H.S. "So, the competitiveness of others brings up your own self-judgement towards your own failure to date to achieve more than you have achieved?"

H.S. "Yes."

H.S. "In what area do you feel that you have most under achieved?"

S.H. "Material success probably. Financial."

H.S. "If you had would you be happier now?"

S.H. "I am not sure, maybe."

H.S. "If this is the case then it would infer, that you associate having money with having more happiness. Is that correct?"

S.H. "Yes and no. I do not believe that money makes you happy."

H.S. "Do you see yourself as a successful man?"

S.H. "In some ways yes."

H.S. "In what areas do you feel you have not been successful?"

S.H. "I do not feel, I have achieved anywhere near my own potential. I realise parts of my character have held me back. However, I also feel that I have done well to achieve much of what I have."

H.S. "You still have a long time to achieve your goals my son. Do not be so hard on yourself. Be patient and continue to trust in your true self. Do not measure or compare yourself to others. They have their own journey and you, your own. No one knows the paths others have trod. How they have achieved what they have achieved. This life is not a competition. This is the mistake of others who let competition rule their lives. There is no one else to compete against in truth. The illusion is that there is 'ANOTHER'. Competitive people only compete in truth with themselves. How can you win when there is no one else to beat? You are then chasing an invisible horse, so to speak. You are deluding yourself to take part in a perpetual race that can never be won. If it can never be won, also it can never be lost. You have woken up my son. That is your greatest achievement to date."

S.H. "I am struggling a bit again at this awful news now, about the current state of the world and the stupidity of some of the major world leaders and their actions and statements. I am concerned about the prospect of a major war breaking out to be honest as I am sure, so are many other people now.

I find it hard to switch off from the media. This is because I do not want to ignore current affairs. I know the price of being aware of world events, is the major cause of my concerns."

H.S. "My son, thank you for sharing your concerns.

Yes, my son you could ignore all the media. However, we appreciate that this is now very difficult in your age. In the future, this era in which you now live, will be called the 'media age', because of the interconnectivity that computers and television provide. The news is instant.

We would suggest to you, a careful choice of what media you connect with, whether audio or visual or written in the same way that you are so careful to protect your physical health, to also protect your mental health. The same vigilance is required here. No matter how difficult or tempting to look at them. Certain publications use fear to draw you in. Avoid all that uses fear to draw your attention towards same. This alone reflects the level of consciousness of the persons or company providing it. For fear, begets fear and love, begets love. The unwise decisions of some of your leaders are being caused by their own misconceptions about situations. Also, their own fears of course from what they see, hear and read themselves.

Here lies your power in your choice of what you ingest mentally, in relation to such issues. This applies to all beings of course.

Continue to reflect love and positivity to all. Continue with your work as you are doing now to spread this message of peace, love and wisdom, to others, whoever may see and read these words. Your world is on the precipice of real change my son, some for the better some for the worse. You will know where to be at such times. Follow your own intuition and instincts as always to guide you and to help lead others where you can. You are safely held now and always in the arms of God. Trust this always my son. Remember this and have no fear. There is nothing to fear, except fear itself. For fear is an illusion of a lie. The lie being that you are but mortal, when in fact you are immortal in your soul and your soul holds no fear. Let your soul be your pilot always my son."

S.H. "Is this why there so much stress and mental illness now. It would appear to be getting worse in some societies?"

H.S. "This is for many reasons my son. Mental illness comes in many forms and yet all are caused by fear. This is fear of many things. Yet fear is fear. Anxiety is caused by fear usually but it is also caused by an individual doing or acting in a way or being treated in a way which does not resonate with his or her own spiritual essence.

The spiritual essence of all beings resonates harmoniously with peace. Peace is your natural state of being. When you are not at peace within, then your body will experience stress. Anxiety is stress of the mind. This is simply your mind not being in a state of peace. When you can return your mind to the present moment, peace will always be available to you. In the present moment, you will resonate most with the essence of your being. Your essence does not reside in the past or the future. Only your mind goes there. Your essence resides in the eternal present moment. It cannot be anywhere else. For this reason, it is the only place to access the peace which you crave."

S.H. "Why is it, that I cannot find peace in my mind but only through my eternal essence by being in the present moment?"

H.S. "Because your mind is not who you are. Your body is not who you are. Your true essence is who you are!"

S.H. "What is my true essence then?"

H.S. "Your true essence is your spirit, your soul. The divinity within you which is eternally connected to that force which you call God. It is the ocean of your being which you are truly.

Your body and mind is this essence experiencing being in the physical world in human form. Through being in this form you are each experiencing all the challenges that such an experience brings. Only through mastery of your body and mind, bringing them both into harmony with the spirit of your essence by living in the eternal present as much as possible will you experience your true nature and its greatest potential. This is why creative activity such as that which you are involved in at this moment allows this presence to flow at its greatest degree. It is because you are connected and immersed putting your own mind to one side allowing it to be free to act as a conduit for the higher awareness of your Higher-Self which is connected with Great Spirit."

S.H. "Thank you."

S.H. "Last night I watched a documentary on the television called 'The Secret', it was about the laws of attraction. It was about obtaining material things or drawing to oneself a relationship with another person. It felt somewhat selfish to me. It was all about self, rather than the greater good. Yet, such laws I do believe to be true, for example, that we create our reality according to our beliefs. The programme however, focused mainly on the use of a universal law, which I suspect only a few are aware of, which could be used for the improvement of society but was instead in my opinion, mostly referred to simply to obtain more money and possessions."

H.S. "My son we take your point, however in making people aware of the greater truth of their own reality or nature, is a good thing is it not?"

S.H. "Yes indeed, the film highlighted that we are part of a universal energy field. All connected. That the universe will provide our wishes like a magic genie if we use our mind and thoughts to visualize and imagine what we wish to bring into our lives and that it will be materialized sooner or later. Whether it be material, health wise or a new relationship. That we should for instance, focus on being healthy rather than focus on our ailments. It did serve as a good reminder of similar information I had read previously."

H.S. "Yes my son. Dependent on the evolvement of the individual, so will it be inherently used. Whether to serve oneself or others, it does not ultimately matter. As long as no harm comes to others. Do not be in judgement of others on this issue my son, as all are evolving at their own pace and in their own time."

S.H. "I have just let go of let go of three old 'friends', as I have just taken three figurines, all native American Indian chiefs, which looked rather like shaman, to a charity shop to be sold on. They were like old friends to me. I acquired them all during a time of great personal sadness and inner turmoil. That time has now passed. They had become instead, a reminder of that difficult period. I felt it was time to let them go. I felt it was also time to let go of the residual personal pain connected to those past difficulties. They were a reminder to me whenever I looked at them to dig deep within myself and to connect with my inner warrior and my own inner strength and wisdom."

H.S. "Those items my son, also represented to you as well as a time of inner turmoil, one also of great change. A great shift took place within you all during the time which those small figurines represented.

You have and are to a degree now the embodiment of that shift and change to the consciousness they represented to you. You have become it and live it daily to the best of your ability, most of the time my son. However, they had become a reminder of past difficulty and pain. You had reached the point that you no longer choose to have such a reminder. This is good my son. Wherever you can release inner pain it will set you free. Make you lighter in body, spirit and emotions. There will be less obstacles in your path to prevent you to achieve your goals that you now desire. Such as the completion of this project 'Awakening to Love'. Bravo!"

S.H. "I do feel a sense of self-empowerment, just from letting go of these objects which were so cherished at the time."

H.S. "This comes from the fact that you knew within, that you had released enough of your inner pain to release them. You knew that the knowledge and wisdom, of which they were a reminder, is embodied and embedded now within your own deepest being. Your own inner strength and security has enabled such a release. Not only that, but the desire that they will be passed on to others and that in some way they will help those who acquire them in the future. Due to the fact, the objects have been passed on in such a sacred way, including how you mentioned some of your story to the staff in the charity shop. This energy will draw only those to these objects who can benefit in a similar way."

S.H. "Good I am pleased to hear that. I am slightly embarrassed making so much mention of what seems on the surface, simply like taking a few personal items to a charity shop. But they represented something very big and important which happened to me in my life.

I want now, only reminders of joy and to feel joy as much as possible. Not reminders of pain, whether it be emotional or physical."

H.S. "Yes my son and this in its own way represents growth on your part, that you are choosing joy over pain which has been your pattern for quite a while has it not my son."

S.H. "Yes it has. Letting go of our past pain and emotional trauma. It is so obvious that it can only be good for us. Why can it be so difficult to release it?

I know from my own experience it can be carried around embedded in our minds, hearts and bodies for years."

H.S. "The mind my son. The mind. It is the mind which keeps you there. Which takes you back. The mind will set you free or imprison you. It is but a choice. A choosing of: - do I choose pain? Or do I choose peace?

Each of you must decide in each moment that the thought or the memory arises!

Some choose the pain out of self-pity or with the desire others will sooth their own pain. You all need to find the source of your own love within. The fact that you are all loved. That you are love. That you are the source of love. So, each time a memory of past pain arises. Choose peace. Choose to feel your own love within your own hearts. You can always find it by unlocking it and this is done by letting go of the pain. This is done by choosing peace which is the love inherent within all. Awaken to that love in each moment simply by choosing it!"

S.H. "I am back here writing after a six week break from this book project. Now I am back in my old haunt to produce these words. The autumn is upon us and as usual I am somewhat lost for a relevant question.

The past six weeks have seen a lot of turmoil on the worlds stage. I myself, not alone for sure, have found it difficult at times not to feel anxious about the threat of a major nuclear war breaking out between North Korea and the United States of America. What can you say about this?"

H.S. "My son, what is it you fear most about these events?

Is it not change, uncertainty pain and death?

Not just for yourself but also for your own family and the rest of humanity likely to be affected?"

S.H. "Yes indeed. I feel selfish at times that my family are at the top of my list of concerns. But I suppose this is a natural way of thinking about such things?"

H.S. "Indeed my son. Your question is reflective of the general state of mind of many in your world at this time. Our main suggestions would be as follows; -

1) Accept what is, but be in the moment.
2) Keep your attention firmly rooted in the present rather than fear for the future.
3) Be grateful for what you have now, that you cherish in your life.
4) Know the greater power that is God, is aware and watching your world.

Although humanity has free will, it will be stopped from self-destruction.

The scenario of which you speak and which is slowly being played out is about the projected fears of some people in positions of power. This power has been given to those that wield it and have allowed these events to come about. These people will be stopped when people choose differently as to whom they choose to govern them. This is not advocating violence to affect change but a peaceful resolution towards change."

S.H. "Thank you. I am also interested to know if the thoughts and emotions of people are affecting our weather now?

By this I mean extreme weather which has been going on for some time? Or is it perhaps down to global warming?"

H.S. "My son, some aspects of your weather are affected by both simultaneously. The hurricane about which you are currently thinking i.e. Hurricane Irma is a natural event. However, the consciousness of the planet also is involved in this event. The effects of the weather on property and persons is not instigated with any thoughts of malice or revenge or anger on the part of the mind of your planet.

However, the effects of such destructive weather events do bring about a change to the consciousness of those affected by these weather events. The usual result is to impart a greater degree of empathy and sympathy towards the hardship of others. They help to soften the hearts of humanity where there is greatest need for this to be instilled. The same is true through acts of war for similar reason. The usual outcome from the effects of war is to imbue greater peace and compassion in the hearts and minds of those in the regions most affected by acts of war. Nothing occurs as you know by coincidence. Those who live by the sword will die by the sword. Those who start wars will suffer the most. Those caught up in such events have chosen to incarnate there at such times for their soul's evolution. Either through the turmoil they experience or through the help to off-set such, through their soul's presence in such places at such times in your history. We cannot predict the future as to what will happen as many different scenarios can unfold. It depends on which one's humanity chooses in your time frame. Continue as you are doing to send out peace and love to all those involved. Choose peace in each moment. REMEMBER that you always have the power to choose peace in each moment. Especially, when you find yourself in an anxious state or place choose peace within your own mind."

S.H. "I was reflecting recently on something which happened to me thirty years ago during a distant healing from person I knew at that time. He was an elderly gentleman and a healer, who my wife at the time, visited occasionally.

I felt something for the first time in my life then, a surge of very powerful energy go up through my spine and it felt as if it was going out of the top of my head and although it was with such benevolent force I felt as though the top of my head was going to blow off, though knowing it would not of course!

It was only in recent times that I have concluded and now believe that what occurred was what is known as a kundalini awakening. (This is when a surge of spiritual energy passes up through all the chakras from the base of the spine up to the crown chakra).

On reflection, this was the start of my own spiritual awakening. Can you comment on such occurrences please?"

H.S. "My son, indeed this was the nature of the event which occurred at that time. It did initiate an awakening and healing within your being. It occurs when the individual is ready in a given lifetime. It does not occur to everybody within any given lifetime. It is quite a rare event. It is an incidence of the soul's awakening to the higher consciousness latent or dormant within the mind of the individual concerned. The force, or presence of the consciousness is always latent within the individual and all around. However, the individual soul is often unaware of it being present within themselves. Such events as you experienced is indeed the start of an awakening and a remembering of the conscious presence within all beings. When this occurs, there is also an activation of various dormant energy centres beyond the Chakra's which are fired up. For example, there are mini-chakras within the hands. These are also activated when the energy starts to flow freely through the individual's bodily system.

Love is the key to this activation within the individual. An openness, an acceptance of the energy is a pre-requisite for the awakening of the individual concerned. It is also by the grace of God that such occurs. The energy revitalises the bodily system including the brain/mind collective of the receiver allowing a shift to occur within the mind-set of that individual. This energy shift prompts a change in the DNA also of the body of the person. The double helix is strengthened and telomeres are strengthened also and revitalised. Meditation practice will continue such benefits, whenever practiced with focus on the divine love inherent within each soul. Let your intention and honourable motivation for global peace guide this energy to the greatest benefit for human kind.

There is occurring at this time a global awakening of soul's as never seen before in the history of your planet. This is the reason so many are incarnated in human form at this time in your history. This is in part, because the souls concerned seek the opportunity of such a spiritual awakening, now on your planet of choice. Your planet Earth is the only planet of choice. Your planet is an experiment, if you like, for the free will of your species. You all have free will to choose your own destiny as individuals and as a race. The human race has not occupied your planet long in the lifetime of your planet itself. The earth has seen so many life forms come and go in its lifetime so far. You are here to embed the mind of God within the minds of men in an awakened state collectively, so that you might be co-creators in the divine plan for your universe. The divine plan being the emergence of God awakened within the race of man to build heaven on Earth and beyond. It is a divine challenge. But it is possible."

S.H. "So is this the purpose of life and why we are here on planet Earth?"

H.S. "The purpose of life my son? Another way of asking the question is 'why does anything exist'?

The alternative is a vacuum. Nothing. Nothingness is impossible. This is because for nothing to be the state of all, it would require that God did not exist. God is all there is. All is contained within the mind of God. There is nothing outside of God. All the good and all the bad, all is within the mind of God. God contrary to opinion is not judgemental. This is left to individuals, if they choose to be so!

So, the reason for life, is that God exists and is eternal. You and all creation, share the essence of God, as a droplet of the ocean shares the ocean. That is why you are here. You are the embodiment of the divine essence of God in human form, as are all beings. Your soul has chosen this body at this time for many reasons. Some for your growth, some for the growth of others. All growth is shared. Part of the reason is to awaken to the level of consciousness revealed here within the pages of this book. Otherwise you will be sleep walking through life. The analogy used is sound and actual, for just as a person can sleep walk, their awareness is barely functioning. A person asleep to their true identity of being, is going through their day to day life in a similar way. The soul awakened in human form is like the comparison of the person awake from slumber and therefore so much more aware of the life around them."

S.H. "This book I hope will awaken others who read it, to their true nature, as you are stating it to be here and I believe it to be. Beyond these words and my everyday activities, how can I increase or amplify the pace of the awakening in others?

My motivation here is, in part, that I feel I can help in and with the transition to a higher consciousness of others. Also, because part of me is impatient to see the fruits of such a shift in consciousness on

Earth. By this I mean that the world becomes more peaceful and a healing occurs where it is needed to the Earth and its environment."

H.S. "My son. We congratulate you on not just your endeavours here, but also the compassion that you feel to improve the lives of others, by helping to bring about this shift. Your presence here and the presence of many others like you at this time helps to activate the shift and change in others. You all carry a frequency within your own energy field which helps to shift and change other persons and places in a way unseen to you. Do not focus on the end result. Instead focus in the given moment on any task at hand. However humble, even when washing up alone in your kitchen. Be in the moment, be present, be peaceful whenever you can and your energy will be radiated to those in need. Know that the frequency of love and harmony affects much in unseen ways. All you need to do is trust that what is meant to be, will be. Do not be attached to any results of your making. In any case, God is the doer. Be the divine witness and loving presence which you are and that you bring into your world."

S.H. "How would you advise others to find their own gift. Especially those who want to raise their own spiritual awareness and go on to help others or make this world a better safer world in which to live?"

H.S. "To go within. Ask to be shown where the gifts lie. Most will be aware in their own hearts where their gifts and skills lie. They will be drawn to be and help in the places and areas where they can grow and help others most. Follow their hearts towards that which they are drawn and to trust in their own intuition. Their own inner teacher my son."

S.H. "Thank you. Yes, following on from that about how brightly our own light shines, because we are also human beings, our light varies from day to day like a dimmer switch makes the light inside a house go up and down in frequency. I guess in a similar way our light is always there but goes up and down at times?"

H.S. "Yes my son, indeed it does. Again, do not be attached to what you give out but the help you can give to others in many ways. Perhaps, just listening, perhaps running an errand for them. Being part of a community means just this."

S.H. "Most people I guess are so caught up in their everyday material lives that they don't have much time, or for whatever other reason, choose just not to think about spiritual matters or the bigger questions?"

H.S. "This is true in many cases, not all of course. There are so many distractions in your world. The focus of your world and many of your governments is on consumerism. This is to make your countries and certain individuals rich. In part for wealth and in part for power. Countries are competing against each other instead of working in harmony together. It is because of this competition, between governments, that so much damage is being done to your environment. It is also the cause of so much of your poverty. The human race is not seen as one family by so many of you. In a simple sense, you are all living in one house. If the house is destroyed, there is no other house which you can move to. You have only one planet. Greed is caused in part, through a prevalent belief that you only have one life time and many use this as an excuse for their own greed and selfishness. Giving at the same time insufficient thought to the fact that future generations, even of their own families will inherit the world and its condition in which it is left. They also are led by their own logical rationale, not realizing they have access to a greater wisdom which resides in the heart. This heartfelt wisdom, comes from the higher wisdom latent in the soul of their being. The captain of their ship. When the captain is ignored too often the ship will hit the rocks as you know too well my son.

People must learn to have the humility to let go to their own perception of their own intelligence with which they are too often smitten. This to their own detriment and often to others. Your greatest wisdom will come to you at those moments when any of you are firmly rooted in the present moment. Allow the currents of wisdom and intelligence to drift in and out of your own conscious awareness. That awareness is like the sky. Your own thoughts and emotions are like the clouds which pass across it. Do not be attached or disturbed by such which bring distress in thought or feeling for they are not you. You are the conscious loving eternal presence as is the sky to the clouds which come and go. Be peaceful. Choose peace always. Remember that. When you are at peace your highest guidance will come to you like a bird on the wing upon the sky. The conscious living presence holds all wisdom and will speak to you on those higher loving frequencies of being when you are tuned in to them. When you need inner guidance ask and it will be given to you. Trust the information and guidance. Be open to how it may be received. God or the divine presence, of all that is, will always serve you. For it is you and you are it. Your inner knowingness is your higher mind. Information will come to you in 'lumps' of 'knowingness,' learn to recognise these. Thought at this level is different to the human thinking to which most are used to. Do not think that that is the only way to think. For it is not. Divine thought and inspiration like the speed of light operates on a different frequency.

Yes, 'egoic' thought, you may call your regular thought patterns such, if you like i.e. thought which stems from the ego, rather than the highest level of your being. Your intuition is affiliated to this highest thought. Your true way of knowing and how truth is communicated to you through your own heart. Follow your heart always. Do not hurt others wherever possible my son, unless in self-defence at times for example of mortal danger. If you follow your highest instincts, this should not be realized in any case.

You can create your own reality with your own thoughts,

words and deeds. You can amplify these with your own powerful imagination also. This is the secret. To your own power and all others. But, always use them kindly, benevolently for yourself or others. Use them always for upliftment of your world. Endeavour always for this and teach by example. 'Namaste', my son."

S.H. "Awakening to the divine consciousness which we all share, is something which I am most grateful for and hold dearly in my heart. The purpose of this book is primarily to help others wherever possible awaken to their own divinity and the unity of consciousness which we all share. This is not only to enrich their lives but also the lives of those around them and for the upliftment of their communities towards a more peaceful way of living."

H.S. "Yes my son. It is easy in the depths of the human experience to forget or remain ignorant of this truth. Many are not interested to go within. Many are more interested in the perception of their exterior world. Many see themselves as being on a singular experience upon your world i.e. that they have the one lifetime and endeavour to get as much material gain for themselves or their own families. To travel and enrich themselves with material things. Many are happy to live this way only. In the main these are people who have yet to realise that this will in the end not bring them real happiness or peace. Accept this. Allow this. When the individual is ready to grow, then they will seek the information, that you readily seek to share with others, contained upon these pages. However, the truth is in each moment available to all, if they but look within and listen to their own inner voice, their own deep inner feelings which arise in the heart of their own truth. Often it takes some sort of personal calamity of pain and suffering to endeavour the change which denotes a change of course along this path of truth.

The steps towards spiritual enlightenment can either be very short or very long. Very easy or very arduous, it depends on the student concerned. Many paths lead to this realising of the true essence of being. That awareness, that they are not alone but held always, in the comforting embrace of the benevolent and loving power of God. The divine oneness of being which all share."

eight

The Planetary Shift
in Consciousness

S.H. "We are living in what feels to many as slightly strange and surreal times. For many this is a scary or anxious time to be alive. I feel concerned for people who suffer with anxiety, which is so common now. So much negative press reporting and media coverage is likely to exacerbate their condition. I am also concerned that peace in the world feels rather unstable as I write."

H.S. "My son, it is understandable that many in your world feel a sense of unease and concern at the lack of seeming stability in your world. It is as if your world were to be likened to a medium sized but slim tree. It is as if every now and again the tree is being shaken vigorously and emotionally, many of you need to cling on to avoid the peril of falling from the tree. The tree is the symbol for your safety, your safe haven so to speak. All the while you know that the tree is not really that safe. Just as in the same way life is precarious and fragile at times, is it not?

You cling to the tree as it shakes also as if it were a tremor or an earthquake. Such events in your world will unfortunately increase due to the 'fear' factor. Fear fuels instability in your physical world in the same way as the emotions of such fuel disharmony within the body. After all the Earth is the body of the world and humans are all like cells within it. They are like the gut bacteria is to the human body. Normally they bring joy but sometimes upset.

Back to the analogy of the tree. What we would suggest that instead of feeling as if you were holding on to the tree, upon one of the branches, think of yourself as the tree itself. Allow yourself to move easily and freely with the wind, do not try to resist the emotions which arise when events occur. Allow them, witness them. Be the witness to them, remembering all the time that you are not them. Knowing that the feelings will pass. Just as the storm will pass. You are not the storm, do not identify yourself with it. Merely be the witness to it.

Your world itself is experiencing a hurricane of emotions. This in turn will continue to manifest storms and earthquakes upon your planet, wherever fear is greatest and other calamities. These calamities have a greater cleansing purpose. Old consciousness is being peeled from the veneer of humanity to reveal a new more enlightened consciousness. This cannot come to the surface until the old consciousness has left the planet, from those very few areas where it remains. Those such areas are not surprisingly revealed, where conflict, chaos and planetary disturbance are most prevalent. Wherever consciousness is held back by fear and fear has the upper hand, so conflict and chaos will manifest. This is so, because of the absence of love in those places in sufficient degree to allow it to take the upper hand.

Yet fear is its own undoing. As it is removed, so it will be replaced in time with a higher consciousness based on love and mutual respect. This is the way life continues for only love has the wisdom sufficient, to ensure survival in the long term my son."

S.H. "So many of the world's problems seem to me to spring from our consumer lifestyle and that which under pins it. This globalisation of the economy will inevitably lead to inequality in so many areas of life. It is really the winner takes all philosophy of life. It is a non-compassionate way of life in my opinion. It breeds competition in all areas and brings out the worst in so many. Its survival also necessitates the continuity of the suppression of strong spiritual belief I believe being propagated in this world, because the teaching adhering to it in the main is about love, compassion, sharing and helping others. It is as if we need a spiritual/political revolution based on the premise that we are all connected as one loving, compassionate family treating all as such and caring for each other regardless of colour, class, nationality."

H.S. "Indeed my son. Well said. That is the direction humanity is moving towards. The infraction and disturbance are being caused by the resistance to the movement in that direction. For example, the resistance towards the idea of global warming and the destruction it causes is being brought about by the greed and self-interest of a few countries to the detriment of many others. As consciousness shifts to higher and higher levels this greed and selfishness will melt away. The warming of the planet will have many benefits over time though not apparent at this time. Global warming, though not caused in or with good intent will bring good to many. Although it will be painful and difficult for many at times of such caused transition. This is a time to bring to the fore, yours and others skill learnt in dealing with and accepting change. Be flexible in all areas. Acceptance is the key word. Trust is the key action. Be it one of attitude, your actions and those of others of a compassionate nature will be defined by their trust in the divine intelligence inherent in and available to all."

S.H. "I know that this global shift in consciousness is well under way and has been for quite a long time. Many people have woken up to their true nature i.e. that they are in truth a spiritual being occupying human form and that everything is interconnected.

Many are already on-board and the ship has set sail. Where it has set sail to, I don't quite know. Hopefully its destination is a better more compassionate world, in our near future?"

H.S. "Yes, you could say that. That is a fair analogy of the current state of play on your planet. You each have and hold a different role wherever or whenever it can be self-realized. Like soldiers going into battle some will realize their goal others will not. It does not matter of course in the greater scheme of things. However, we know that it matters to you my son. You do have a competitive nature and you do not like to be beaten. In this case, your only opponent is yourself. You cannot win or lose. That is not possible. Instead, just be and trust that your highest dreams will be realized. Do not allow the ego to stand in your own way. Allow the humility of love and support of the divine consciousness to guide you always, it will not let you down in your endeavours to put your message across to many. Remember this message is already known within the hearts of many and the latent knowingness has been there always for all humans. You are simply helping them to remember what they already know, yet often, not trusting or believing in that inner knowingness within themselves.

We have been filling your world with the vibrations of this birthing change for eons of time. Just like a switch, the frequency has been increased because the physical bodies you now possess have undergone sufficient change to accommodate this increased or raised frequency of consciousness. Too much too soon would cause many great impairment to their mental health. This is because their bodies, let alone the minds of most could not accommodate such rapid change. This is because the bodily vibration was too slow, too heavy to house, to accommodate it. It is no coincidence that so many, especially the younger generation are turning away from a diet based on meat and dairy. As they turn away also, from drugs and alcohol in many cases. This also, is caused largely by the increased vibration of their bodies and they know intuitively that these products and substances will not only cause harm to their minds and bodies but also for other ethical reasons of a spiritual nature. Your planet has been reprogrammed to shift. It is not just the human population of the planet but also the consciousness of Earth itself which has been and is continuing to be raised by these loving vibrations of the divine. It is also affecting the rest of life on Earth to varying degrees.

Those of you who do not accommodate these new energies will be left behind. The souls of such will choose at a deep level to leave their current incarnation and continue elsewhere, where they feel more at home with their current state of evolution.

The world therefore is undergoing a cleansing of the lower vibrational frequencies in whatever bodily form they adhere to or occupy. This is what is causing so much of the conflict, pain and suffering you see within pockets of the planet. It will not last much longer in your time. Within the next few decades it will be cleared away. A long period of peace on Earth will follow."

S.H. "I have through the course of much of my adult life called on my own faith and the use of meditation to help me during my own difficult times. I have had to learn to go within and to face my own fears and doubts, to build confidence in my own self and to appreciate my own self-worth. I only mention this now, because if I could, I would like to pass some of what I have learnt to help others who face similar issues. However, I know that this can be a difficult thing to do, perhaps this can only be resolved through the lessons learnt by those individuals by and for themselves?"

H.S. "Yes, to a certain extent this is true. The information you suggest is subjective, the experience of suffering mental torment through the fear and anxiety caused by self-imposed and distressing thoughts is the objective experience of only the beholder of such thoughts and emotions. Though common to many the individual needs to learn for themselves that they are the channel, through which the thoughts pass. They are not the thoughts, they are not their emotions. They are like the still mountain lake, reflecting the mountains on a clear day. Their consciousness acts a bit like the surface of the lake. It reflects that around the surface but the images which appear on it are not of the lake. They are but reflections. These reflections come and go, as your thoughts come and go too.

In the same way, your divine consciousness will only reflect truth to you when it is calm and undisturbed. You will not be able to see or feel the divine truth unless you are calm within.

The techniques you have learnt are all methods using the analogy of the still lake surface, ways in which to achieve this within your own self. By calming your mind and emotions the lake surface or divine consciousness can reflect the truth. In the same way, the mind is disturbed through inner conflict, as is the surface of the lake when the wind and storms ensue across its surface and the reflection of what is real i.e. in this case the peaceful reflections of the mountains, cannot be revealed until calmness returns.

You are not the storms or the peaceful reflection. Your consciousness is neither the lake surface for all are temporal. They all come and go. But here is the paradox of what you are trying to explain to others. Your thoughts which cause you trouble, disturb your inner peace. You battle each time to regain it by calming the surface of your own inner lake. For a while it is calm. Reflections of truth appear to stabilise and calm your inner being. Then the cycle is repeated time and again. You would like the cycle to stop. You would like the surface of your inner lake to be calm always. Do you not?"

S.H. "Yes."

H.S. "But this of course is not possible in your earthly experience. The events which cause the disturbance to the inner lake surface, whatever the cause, will always come and go. The secret is to remember that you are all of that. You are the disturbances, by that we mean you cause them but you are not them. Do not identify with them. You are not even the lake surface which changes and comes and goes. You are the awareness which views the calm or the storm. You are the witness of the lake surface. You are not the surface.

In your own self when you sense all is at peace and all is calm, you are not that peace and calm for you are also in a sense the storm too or so it seems to you. The only thing to identify yourself with is the conscious presence or witness to both.

Like the human, you stood at the shore of the lake looking on, watching all of this. You see the storms, stillness and reflections of the mountains. You see them all come and go upon the surface of your own inner lake. You are the witness to all this but you are not it!

You are the divine eternal witness observing it all. That is the real essence of you and all."

S.H. "To continue then. This is a very subtle process of differentiation of what we see as our everyday consciousness i.e. the idea that we are the feeling and thinking we identity our being with. Rather than this more unified mysterious presence of divine consciousness deep within our being."

H.S. "Yes, my son and I will tell you why. It is because you are so caught up in your own thoughts and emotions as are the vast majority of people, that you do not realize the greater you. All your teaching is towards identification with the body and all its inner processes. That it is not possible to be separate, or greater than that. That there is no connection between all of creation. You are not taught otherwise. Therefore, fear ensues, for you are effectively brought up to believe that you are all an island of individuality, cut off from the rest. Easily abandoned and alone. This is the greatest fear of so many my son. Yet the opposite is true. You can never be truly abandoned or alone for you can never be annexed from your real self, which is the divine presence which animates all creation. This is the intelligence which has brought life to all in your world and throughout all creation. In truth, this is too great for the mind to comprehend fully. Imagine being aware of every thought, every feeling and every emotion of all humans at one time. It would be impossible. The human mind is designed to have its focus only on the one individual for your sanity. The divine mind does not have this problem."

S.H. "So as our consciousness shifts we see the things we saw before, from a totally new perspective. This allows change to occur in our lives."

H.S. "Yes, as this new consciousness grows in the minds of many the change will peacefully emerge and the old ways of thinking will die out. The new will replace the old. This is the way it has always been. The group mind is reflected to the rest. Those fighting the change will disappear in time. They represent the old ways based on fear and intransigence. They are trying to hold on but it will be to no avail. They do not want true peace to prevail. They are not comfortable with it because it does not serve their belief system. They do not want to change. They know that the only way they can have more than others is to keep many in poverty. To feel successful themselves they need to feel that they have more power or possessions than others. For this is how they measure their own self-worth by the measures of the material world rather than the spiritual world. This is because they have no belief in the spiritual world which they believe is just a lie. It is also why they think that there will be no consequences for their actions which are harmful to others. So, in this lifetime as long as they survive they think themselves invincible to retribution. But just as the seasons pass which are unstoppable, so is the season of their being. For a new season of enlightenment is dawning. The darkest hour is often before the dawn my son."

S.H. "One of the biggest challenges humanity is facing now is global warming and the changes it brings to many people's lives. Is it being caused by man or is it being caused by natural phenomena?

I watched a television programme last night, as I write, about the permafrost melting in Siberia which is releasing methane gas into the atmosphere. This is apparently more potent than carbon dioxide gas with its global warming effect."

H.S. "My son we can confirm global warming is real. It is being caused by a combination of factors. Some are caused naturally by light and heat emitted by your Sun. Human activity is also having an effect. This will have an array of huge effects on your planet. Some will assist human kind. Some of the effects will hinder. It will lead to a decrease in your earth's population of human beings. It is not good for the well-being of humanity in general as overall it will make life more challenging. It is not bad per se. It depends on the perspective of the individual affected.

Humanity will be forced to change the way they live and be more mindful of your planets eco-system on which you depend. Just like your own body, the body of Earth needs to be lovingly cared for to survive in a way it can embrace the types of life found on Earth at this time.

The judgement that you are considering as to whether it is good or bad is based on the human perspective of experience. Humanity does not own or rule the planet. That lies in the hands of the greater consciousness which you all share."

nine

A Time of Change

S.H. "So, how do I remain calm, while all the others are 'losing their heads', so to speak, being anxious about such potentially worrying things?"

H.S. "My son, as we have told you so many times, you have but to go within, to that place of peace within yourself. Even when in the centre of the storm peace can be found. It is to be flexible at all times and not to resist change. Whatever the nature of change that appears. You all deal with change in different ways my son. Some fear it, some embrace it. We do not recommend that you should do either. However, we do recommend that you accept change always.

Firstly, what is change really. We would suggest to you that change is movement. As you move through time, different opportunities inevitably arise. Some you might take and others you might decline to take for various reasons. The one's which you are most likely to take up are the one's which you yourself have either called for or created on some other less conscious level. Each change reflects a new challenge or test of your greater self which enables the possibility of growth of your inner being towards mainly greater and greater wakefulness. This being in the sense, of the consciousness of the individual as to who they really are. Whether you are aware of this being the journey or not is another matter. This applies to all. This is because life's course, whichever it takes always leads to this ultimate gaol or purpose. This is simply because it is the reflection of the true purpose of life, which is firstly to awaken to who you really are. Then in time when all of humanity has awakened in your future you will co-create your world, your planet consciously with God. Until that time, the true healing will not occur. This is because mankind in its current mental state is not capable of living this way. This is because humanity, as it stands, thinks primarily of itself, as individuals rather than as one. Selfishness is the inevitable result. When humanity thinks as one, not surprisingly, greater positive change will occur for all. The likes of such, your world as it currently stands, cannot conceive. This is because all decisions will be based in and on love of the highest order for the good of all creation upon your planet. Your current digital age is a precursor for this conscious age to come. It is an 'Awakening to Love' of the highest order. Global warming will assist in this change in ways which humanity cannot yet conceive as they do not know exactly what changes will be brought about by it. As we have already said and it is why, global warming is not necessarily good or bad. It is a wave of change upon which much of this new consciousness will be carried as the old is swept away by it. Accept these changes with grace and fearlessness for in time they will be shown to have helped to heal your world, into what it will become in your future."

S.H. "All around us now we face the prospect of change. Political change and a movement towards a greater sense of materialism and in some cases isolationism. What is the deeper spiritual significance of this, if there is any?"

H.S. "My son, as we have previously said your world on many levels is in a state of flux, greater than ever before. The significance of this change is that the outer is a reflection of the inner physical world of your planetary change and the deeper emotional and mental change within humanity. This encompasses the spiritual recognition of change within those individuals who have a sufficient degree of their own personal awareness about such things. The inner reflects the outer and visa-versa. Humanity is seeking a greater freedom towards free personal expression on all levels. Humanity is more connected to the inner compassion they hold for others. A greater sense of fairness is incumbent upon themselves as regards the treatment of others."

S.H. "If those changes reflect a surge in the raising of human consciousness then would it be logical to assume that as a result our society globally will become a better, more liberated and compassionate society. Although anyone who views the evening news regularly might think that society is getting worse not better?"

H.S. "Yes my son. You might, if your focus relies only on the news feeds, which feed you. Those which keep you afraid and in doing so, disempowered. The rulers still in power are happy with this status quo as it serves their own end's and keeps them in power to protect the interests of those who think along similar lines. Those who seek personal riches and power of a material nature. Those who's focus is not on the many but the few.

The truth lies within you. Be the change that you want to see in the world and others will follow. Lead by example, to others. Be the example you want to see. If you sow kindness and compassion it will grow in others. Through the words of this book you are trying to do just that. Those world leaders who speak kindness and compassion, breed such in others. More and more of your younger generation are more aware and in tune with the messages and the songs of kindness. Their hearts are filled with greater tolerance, kindness and compassion, than many of your own and older generations still alive. The desire by some of your leaders still in power, is to sow disunity and fear to maintain the status quo which they feel most comfortable with, which is based on elitism, greed, power and egotistical thinking. This old way of thinking is based on fear. A fear of lack, a fear of failure. It is based on a sense of emptiness and lack. A lack of belief in the power of the love and divinity that they deny to be within themselves and all others. It is a God-less way of thinking."

S.H. "Yesterday, after my session of writing a section of this book, I went to a talk given by a woman who used to be a war correspondent for the media. After the talk, we were invited to ask her questions about her work. I was curious to know about how she dealt with any stress or trauma caused by the upsetting nature of some of the things she witnessed during her career. She said, 'myself and my colleagues just had a nice meal, a drink and a chat and that sorted it all out'.

Some people however, I believe, are more deeply affected by the things that they witness in their lives on a psychological or emotional level, to cope in such a simple way.

How is stress and trauma best dealt with?"

H.S. "What is stress, what is trauma?

It is a dissonance of disharmony in the individual. It is a temporary lack of peace. Peace and equilibrium need to be restored within the individual being. Whatever brings about the restoration of peace is key. This will be different for each person. However, a conscious decision to choose peace is required.

When peace returns the hormones within the body and brain will regulate themselves, so that the individual feels calm again. The body can withstand periods of stress and trauma, but any regular occurrence should be avoided if possible, as you know."

S.H. "Would you recommend meditation as a good way to deal with stress and trauma?"

H.S. "This is useful if you have developed this method and have acquired the benefits of such. Meditation is more than sitting still for a period of time trying to calm the mind. As you yourself know it can be a demanding practice in itself at times. Many thoughts, fears and anxieties can arise in the space it creates. Many people would find the idea, at a time of worry and trauma as the worst thing that they could practice. However, through your constant practice you have learnt how best to derive benefit through its practice. Also, when is a good time for it and when is not so good a time?

Meditation is in no small part, a practice which requires looking at and dealing with your own fears. This can prove distressing, for many are not ready to do so. To practice meditation, you need to have psychologically reached the point of acceptance of such and preparedness to do so. This is a difficult thing to teach but acceptance of whatever arises is key. Detachment is one of the skills learnt over time. The ability to be detached from what arises and to view it as a witness from a non-judgemental position. This is all part of the acceptance. To go within sounds easy but for many, especially those troubled souls, it takes great courage.

If, meditation therefore, can bring you peace, then yes, it is a good practice for you at such times my son."

S.H. "Some very highly evolved spiritual beings, people, are known to develop a type of 'halo' around their heads. Sri Sathya Sai Baba, the famous Indian Avatar who I saw in India, several times had one. My question is what causes such to appear?

By this I mean in physical terms. I understand it is because they have developed themselves to a high level, in a spiritual sense."

H.S. "My son, this is because of the amount of light that they emit from their essence and being. It is if you like an outer expression of the divinity they carry which has grown so strong that it has become visible in the outer world. It is around the brow and crown chakra's primarily, because this is where the light, it is strongest.

The crown which is worn by royalty is a physical representation of this. It is supposed to infer a mock replacement of the authority conferred from a higher place. A substituted 'halo' not real in the spiritual sense. This is because royal persons knew that such persons, who had attained this highest level of their spiritual development, would also be conferred with this halo of light around their forehead. Royalty are endeavouring to confer the same by wearing their crown. The meaning has been lost through the passage of time. But this is the reason a jewelled crown of gold is chosen my son."

S.H. "Thank you. I have never come across that information before to the very best of my recollection but it makes good sense why a crown is chosen by royalty. Especially at the time of a coronation."

S.H. "Does whatever we listen to, for example, good or bad news in our social and news media affect our health and consciousness in different ways. I would presume that listening to bad or frightening news for many years is bound to affect us all in various ways?"

H.S. "Yes of course. It is in a way no different to what you eat or drink over a long period. In this case, it is what you take in to your mind-consciousness and how it can affect your belief systems.

To a great extent, you are at the mercy of the media if you choose to tune in to it. We suggest that you filter it and chose each time, to what you give your attention to. You do not want unnecessarily to introduce too much anxiety inducing news or programming for the sake of it. It can be addictive out of curiosity, often at times.

Those who suffer a sensitive disposition or who have anxiety or who have mental health issues are the ones who should be most guarded, to what information they regularly expose themselves to.

Choose instead to give your minds to those places and topics which feed and strengthen your minds in more positive ways. Information which uplifts and empowers not only your conscious minds but your physical bodies too. When the mind is feeling positive the physical body therefore reaps the benefit of the many health inducing properties created within your physical bodies as a result. This will make you feel more alive and energised and more able to achieve your goals and to assist others with theirs.

The purpose of your news in most cases is not to indoctrinate more people to be more fearful but this is the affect so often. It is done with lack of forethought of the outcome of such. It is due to a lack of awareness as to its greater effect on many in society. Especially the elderly who have the time and are more likely to listen.

However, with the digital age the information is so readily available to your young people who are becoming more and more effected as a result. There is much positive news as well however. In many cases this is making secrecy more difficult and much that was once hidden, is now no longer possible. The suppression of information about certain matters is now much more difficult.

The consciousness of your society ultimately is the measure of what is most readily shared and devoured in terms of news information and learning. As the consciousness of people raises, so most information most readily shared, will reflect that. In time your society will become more aware of the effects of fear inducing and negative reporting. They will realise that positive news will better the upliftment and create a more compassionate caring society. It is all to do with self-awareness, in truth. It is about being sufficiently present for a sufficient amount of time to be aware of how your media affects your thoughts, emotions and ultimately the health of society in general."

S.H. "The previous question, just asked, came to me yesterday when I was listening to a radio show. This is on the radio every week day and is listened to by millions of people. It is a topical news show reporting on items of news.

The public telephone in and express their views on a great variety of matters. Only occasionally is it a positive spin on some matter or other. In my opinion because of the usually negative topics up for discussion, it seems to just feed societies fears generally held by so many, rather than trying to focus on positive stories, which would be beneficial in so many ways."

H.S. "Yes my son. It is possible of course. When consciousness changes sufficiently, such things will change also. Not until such times. Be the change you want to see in the world."

S.H. "Would it be an accurate analogy to describe the essence of our being i.e. the awareness that we 'truly' are, as being like, someone viewing a television and our human self as being like that television? Then all the things shown on the television in question as being analogous for the dramas and events within our own lives. In the same way, we the viewer or witness are detached from the drama and in a similar way our eternal consciousness, witnesses our day to day lives and dramas."

H.S. "Yes, my son. On a superficial level this is so. The main difference and what you are forgetting, is that it is the same consciousness witnessing all the dramas on all the televisions. Each person identifying only with themselves and their own dramas. There is only <u>one</u> conscious presence or witness to it all. That, at the deepest level, is who you all are. This is why, in furtherance to the conversation that you just had with your friend 'Alex' in the street, a few minutes ago (at the time of writing this), the reason how the 'osmosis' of the 'zeitgeist' works, because there is only one consciousness and you are all it. Therefore, it cannot, not be shared, at the deepest level. Whether or not the individual draws on it, depends on their own level of awareness and the beliefs they hold themselves. This is because they act as a filter to what the individual accepts into their own thought process. Also, their own depth of intuition that they have within themselves."

S.H. "When I try to think about this, it makes me feel like I could go a bit 'crazy', if I dwelt too much on this idea or truth as I am led to believe."

H.S. "Why do you think it could send you a bit crazy?"

S.H. "Because a part of my mind, my rational mind is scared that I might release the rational thought processes that we all have and use daily to function in our usual normal everyday lives. Maybe it is a fear of acting in a way too strange or too different to everyone else. A fear of coming across just a bit too weird and strange.

Ultimately, a fear of what others might think of me. Yet, I know that I can deal with that because I already do speak my truth to those who show an interest in my own spiritual beliefs."

H.S. "Yes, my son. Part of your purpose is to share the wisdom you hold. Do not be afraid to let your light shine. You have much to give and share with others. You have chosen a physical instrument which your soul knew would have a good chance of helping your gifts be brought to the fore. You knew in advance deep in your soul that the journey would not be easy but you hold the courage to do it to the best of your ability to help others also grow in awareness. This is your gift. It is part of the reason why you are writing this book."

S.H. "Yes, thank you for those kind words. I have had an anxious time these last few days. When I return to that anxious space within myself, it is also a reminder of how far I have come, about how I feel now most of the time, generally feeling good and less anxious within myself.

I would like now to understand more fully how this conscious awareness that we all share and truly are, how it connects with the energy of love?

In my own mind, I separate them each time. As if they are two different things. Can you help me understand how and why they are connected in the simplest terms so that I can understand them in unity?"

H.S. "Unity is the key word here to help you understand my son. The one embraces the other. There is no separation. They are the two sides of one coin. The wisdom holds the love and the love holds and embraces the awareness that is the wisdom. The life force is the loving wisdom. You are trying to understand it from a logical perspective instead of standing within it. To know it is to feel it not to think it. To think it is to dissect the two. To feel it is to experience the two together.

The mother holds her child with love. The intelligence within her body without her conscious help has created the baby newly born i.e. love plus awareness (creative intelligence).

If you imagine for a while that you are that mother. You will see no difference between the two aspects. They dance in unison in a loving embrace, love and the creative wisdom which led to the baby's body being born. Some things cannot be explained in words. This is because there are no words, no labels to explain it. That is why the answer you seek to this question needs to be understood by what you feel and not what you think. Thought is a blunt tool when it comes to revealing the essence of the creator. The best way to awaken is to "AWAKEN TO LOVE' and the answer you seek will flow into the divine consciousness shared by you all."

S.H. "So is it correct to say, that whoever the person, who is reading this, at whatever moment in time, that at the deepest level, their awareness is the same awareness that is writing this book in this now moment?"

H.S. "Yes my son that is correct."

S.H. "I am quite excited by this, as I seem myself, to now understand this concept of oneness, and this conscious awareness being shared by all, more than I did before. I thank you so much. It is a joy to be learning more about it."

H.S. "It is a joy for us too. I say, 'us' and I say 'I' to make conversation easier in this context. The truth of the matter is that there is no 'us' and only 'I'. This is because there is only one awareness in all of creation. It is just that it is shared by all, as all are of it, at the deepest level of being. It is just that for most, it is hidden by all the other distractions of physical life."

S.H. "I would like to know how to help awaken as many people as possible, to this universal awareness that we all share.

I noticed yesterday, after going away from my place of writing this book and understanding it more deeply that I felt more love than I do normally for others. This felt as if it was a direct result of that deeper understanding."

H.S. "Yes indeed, it would be that, for that is how it works not surprisingly, that the more the awareness of oneness grows, the more love you feel. The more love you feel the more that wisdom flows also within yourselves. Embrace this truth each day. In the simplest terms, this is the only one truth you need to learn. For all else, will flow from that, which is required in your world to heal all ills my son."

S.H. "Thank you. Yes, I can see how that is possible. That the best way to live, is to stay as much of the time as possible in that higher awareness?"

H.S. "This my son is where self-mastery comes into the equation. As we have already taught you, staying in the present moment as much as possible is key. This involves what many are now referring to as mindfulness. Yet the term of 'mindfulness' is a paradox, as the purpose of the term is meant to mean mind emptying in many ways. Do not be distracted by this, as really staying in the now moment is about being as present as possible. Learning to be able as much as possible to put to one side whatever the distraction might be, whenever you can. There are many skills you can learn to help this process. Meditation is an obvious one. So is yoga, as is exercise. Develop the intent each day to be as present as possible in the 'now' moment as you can. Do not judge yourself however, when you find you cannot do it, for the skill to do so, takes constant practice and determination. The more you can be present the more your creativity will flourish, in whichever way you wish to pursue. We would recommend that ways which help others, will be of most benefit for you personally. This will be for you, reaping the fruit of the seeds which you have sown for so long."

S.H. "So through our awakening to love at a deep level, it is that, which helps us to awaken to the awareness, the consciousness that we all truly are?

Is it correct to say that we do not only share that consciousness which pervades all creation; BUT THAT WE ARE IT?"

H.S. "Yes my son that is correct. However, on top of being that awareness, you are ALL THAT IS!"

For it stands to reason that if that awareness pervades all creation then you are also that, through the connection being the awareness that is present through all."

S.H. "I am starting to more fully comprehend being the awareness within all people but at this moment finding it a bit more difficult to fully comprehend being 'all that is'!"

H.S. "Your mind can only comprehend so much at a time. Allow your comprehension to grow incrementally, naturally. You are so eager to grow in your comprehension my son and that is good. But, it is like a young person who wants to be bigger, older and wiser than they are ready to be, at the time. Allow, yourselves to grow into this greater awareness and it will happen with time. It cannot be forced."

S.H. "I feel as if, for the last thirty years, that I have been struggling with the concept of understanding being part of oneness. I feel a big penny has dropped. I now understand the concept of one awareness better, or of one consciousness that we all share. Despite the fact people are all at different levels in their spiritual awareness. It seems strange, how I could not understand it better before. I think it was the idea I held for so long, that my consciousness was a <u>part</u> of the 'sea of consciousness', rather than <u>the</u> 'sea of consciousness' of all that is.

I myself, on numerous occasions, have used the analogy of the droplet of water and the ocean. In so doing I would say that we are all the ocean and not the droplet. But I realise now, that even though I voiced it to others, that even then, I did not understand the concept, the idea, as I do now. Maybe I was just not ready to understand?"

H.S. "Because you understand it more deeply, you can now feel love more deeply. That is why you feel more love, as you do now my son. This will continue to grow as your understanding grows. This is how it develops. As the love grows. So, the secrets will be revealed, slowly as a flower opening to the sunlight my son."

S.H. "So, the paradox is we all share the same awareness and yet we don't. That is where the difficulty in understanding it, comes in I think."

H.S. "Yes up to a point my son. Take the example of the mother of several children. They all share the same mother but they have a different experience of her being their mother. This is dependent on the thoughts and emotions they have about her. Yet she is the same mother to all. They therefore all have a slightly different experience of her being their mother. So, it is also with the consciousness that you all are. You are sharing it at the same time as being it. Your focus is experiencing it i.e. 'awareness', rather than sharing or being it. This is because you feel outside of it rather than within it. You are starting to see it from within as well as from without i.e. from the outside, so to speak. Do you understand this concept my son?"

S.H. "Yes, I do. I think."

H.S. "Your life is constantly distracting you from who you really are. The truth is almost hidden most of the time. This is natural to ensure the survival of the physical body. This is why to go within, is recommended when you are in suitable space and place and not when you are driving a car for example. Your senses are trained to focus on outside of yourself and not inside. The 'inner- view', reveals the truth of who you are. Yet, this is counter-intuitive to your sense of reason. Yet, this is the path which will reveal who you truly are, if a person persists with such endeavours."

S.H. "I have been reflecting back on my own life and as I write this wondering if I would like to relive it to date if it were possible. This is because much of it, especially when I was a younger adult was very difficult. Compared to many, I know however, that I have been blessed in many ways too. However, I have learnt many things through my own and often self-induced difficulties."

H.S. "My son. As regards this question, although a little self-indulgent, would be common to many. It really depends on how you measure your own life. There will always be others who will enjoy their own lives more than you. In the same way that there will be others who feel that their own has been be-set with more suffering than your own. This cannot be measured only experienced.

We would suggest to you, that the best way to view your life so far, is, how has your own life helped and enriched the lives of others?

Your own pain and suffering has taught you the truth's which you are outlining here in this book. The purpose being to enrich the lives of others. Therefore, any suffering of your own is and has benefited many other people. Your own personal sacrifice of an easier 'ride' in life was consciously chosen by you, to help to ensure the likelihood of your awakening, to help fulfil this purpose. That is to help others to awaken to the spiritual essence within themselves. It was your soul's calling my son. You chose the life you are in with your own higher knowing in advance of some of the likely difficulties which would lay ahead but also many of the benefits and riches in a spiritual sense. It is your own pain which has led in the main to your awakening not you pleasure my son. This is not to say that awakening cannot be found by 'joy' alone. It can, but it was not of your choosing. This is because you had not yet evolved sufficiently to that level of consciousness."

S.H. "Is it more difficult to always be in a space of joy within one's own self than in a space of pain and inner turmoil?"

H.S. "Both are easy. One you must choose. The other you must embrace. You could have chosen to embrace joy. Instead for much of the time, you chose inner turmoil. This was because you did not understand that you had a choice to choose between them. This is because of where you were at, within yourself. It was a reflection of your own level of awareness at any given time. Some use the saying, 'at that time I was in a dark place'. What they mean is that they were in a state of inner struggle, toil and pain. Mental confusion also in your own case. What they fail to realise is that the 'dark place' was of their own choosing, because the light was always present around them but they failed to see it. This is because the pain within their own minds obliterated it from view. This is because the perception was that, what is going on in the mind must be real. In actual fact, it is merely what the individual has chosen to project onto the 'lake surface' of their own awareness. Not realising that they are the

179

awareness, rather than whatever is being projected onto it. You are not your thoughts. You are not your mind. You are consciousness."

S.H. "What is a thought and where does it come from at the deepest level?"

H.S. "A thought is a projection of your own consciousness upon the 'screen' of your mind. The screen, the mind, is temporal. The consciousness is immortal. The thoughts come from your consciousness but they are not of it. Emotions are the main cause of thoughts. Think of an emotion, as being a pebble tossed into lake. It results in one or more ripples. These are the thoughts. The consciousness is the lake. The thoughts are an affect and an effect on consciousness but they are not consciousness itself. However, without consciousness there are no thoughts to be had. The description once again is limited to the availability of the words at hand."

S.H. Through this 'channeling' process that I am now engaged in as I write this book, can you only use words which are stored in my own memory for the answers here, and if so why?

Why can words if so, with their meaning not familiar to me, also be available in the answers here?"

H.S. "The words used, in the main are ones used regularly by yourself. It is because of their familiarity of use that they are 'plucked forth' so to speak and not other words, although they are words for which you know the meaning. They are ones very seldom or never used by yourself. The part of your brain which draws on the use of a large vocabulary, is not one used much by yourself. This is because as you know your life-style at this time, does not include a lot of conversation with others. Say for example you made your living through public speaking, this aspect of your brain's use of vocabulary would be increased."

S.H. "Last night I had a dream which led to me being very upset. It brought up other emotionally painful events which have happened to me during my own life. It revealed to me yet again my own sensitive nature. However, it also reminded me that I am a resilient character, thankfully. A recurring theme to my perceived emotional pain surrounds a feeling of and sometimes a fear of being abandoned in some way by those I love.

One of my ways of coping, at such times is simply to remind myself that at the deepest level, we are all loved. This is because I do believe, we essentially are love and therefore the source of that love. This reminder has helped me a lot at some of my most difficult times in my own personal life. I also know that a lot of the suffering in the world revolves around similar feelings for many other people. A lot of those people do not have the same belief or faith that should enable them to draw on such to help them through their own difficult times. Times when they feel most alone and abandoned.

I would like to help them also to believe that they also, are loved. That they also are love. That they also, are the source of that love.

Can you please say something to add to this or reaffirm it?"

H.S. "My son, indeed you are a sensitive soul. This is a source for much of your compassion for others. It is also why you find it hard to deal with the suffering of others.

You are right in your belief about love. Let me put it another way though:

You are the love, to which eternity rings, truly, for all of creation, throughout your universe.

You are the love, which holds the child, yet not born.

You are the love, on the Eagles wing in the dead of night searching for what it thinks could be its last meal.

You are the love, which within your own hands, hold the sands of time.

You are the love, which springs forth again and again to those who doubt their own truths in their own minds.

You are the love, for those people who when they look in the mirror, only see their own self-hatred and loathing.

You are the love, which sees past their own self-denial and yet still knocks relentlessly at the unconscious, still not awake to who they truly are.

You are the love, which sends out the thoughts and prayers to the leaders of your world, to help to ensure peace and not war. War as you perceive it to be. For war in the minds of many is a holy war. They think that God is on one side only and not the other person's side.

You all, in your own way's make war with your own selves too. Yet even this war is futile. You cannot win a war with your own self. You can only lose. You lose, whoever you make wars against, for there is only you. You are in essence, waging war against yourself and only yourself. For as we have told you, there is only one consciousness, one awareness one true being. All are that. All that is, is what and who you truly are. Sharing your experiences as the one shares all that is with the you that you perceive yourselves to be. This being just a reflection of the tiniest part of the real you.

When you feel, unloved or abandoned try to remember that it is not possible to be separate from all that is. Any more than the wave can be separate from the ocean of its being, even though it feels like it is just a wave, soon to lose its form. It always was the ocean and it always will be!"

S.H. "It must be very liberating to be able to hardly ever think about one's self. I mean as in a selfish sort of way. I would like to be able to do that more. My tendency is to worry basically and usually about myself. I am ashamed to say."

H.S. "My son, you choose your own thoughts in each moment. If you wish to be less self-indulgent in your own thinking, then this is perfectly within your own power if you choose it. However, there will be no point in shifting your worries from your own self to worrying about others. This would be futile and serve no purpose. Instead, what you could do is to think about others only in a constructive way, such as how you can improve the lives of others in your society. If you chose this, the obvious choice would revolve around people with issues that you personally can either relate to most or for whom you feel the most empathy and compassion. Then direct those feelings, to in some way, serving the needs of others. Whoever they should be."

S.H. "So perhaps to summarize, some of the main points of these teachings in relation to awakening, to and through the vibration of love: -

1) We are not the body.
2) We are not the mind.
3) We are all consciousness/awareness.
4) We all share the same ocean of consciousness which permeates all of creation.
5) We are all one.

That oneness goes by many names. One of which is God."

H.S. "That is correct my son. You are an ocean of consciousness gently lapping upon the shores of time. That time is always now.

The eternal present. Your point of contact with this consciousness is always the present moment.

All of this knowledge is of no use to anyone unless they are present as much as possible in the present moment. The present moment is the moment where creation occurs from.

When you are present in the present moment, you are in the true presence of the true you that you and all truly are and which you all truly share.

The skills of living have this as a key purpose to help you be present. The more present you can be, the more life you can bring to each present moment. The more you will be able to be of service in your field of personal contact. The more you and anyone else can serve humanity.

You are love. You all are light. You are the consciousness now awakening to your true nature which never left. It has always been present in the gentle slumber in the mist of humanity's sleeping. Willing your awakening to come at the dawning of this new stage of humanity's being. Through this awakening in this next millennium, humanity will take a greater leap forward than ever before in its evolution. Moving as a large shoal in mindful, instinctual unison in its ocean of being. So, will humanity in its new-found unity, of the oneness of being, discover its own true purpose of being in serving as God's own co-creator in human form, to help seed your universe with a freshly awakened species of humanity acting in a loving wisdom never seen before in your manifest and physical universe."

S.H. "One of my own personal struggles is staying aware of this information.

The sleeping state has an almost gravitational pull like effect, on my awareness. Continually pulling me back into that historical slumber of unawareness. I sort of keep going back and forth. In and out, so to speak in my level of awareness of these truths. Which I do genuinely believe to be true and have believed for a long time."

H.S. "This is normal and the human condition, as the levels of awareness in humanity rise, this will become easier as more people raise their own consciousness.

When the spring follows winter and new growth springs forth the meadows appear all over your globe filled with flowers opening to the sunlight. This is how we see your own awakenings. A thing of beauty to behold by your brethren star-makers. For that is what you are too. It was our loving consciousness which gave birth to all that you see before you. In all this beauty, nothing sprung forth without the deepest aspect of your true being willing to be so present. Visible to your own eyes created like-wise by the same loving benevolent being of conscious eternal loving presence. You are that force. You are that power. You are that wisdom. It is just that, for only an infinitesimal moment of eternity you forgot who you were. Now like one light bulb after another, you are returning to the illumination of your own knowing self. Back, at one with the true nature of the infinite ocean of being which you always were, whom you always will be. Love. Love. Love!"

Printed in Great Britain
by Amazon